Tessa Souter currently lives in New York and performs as a jazz singer throughout the US and Britain. Her critically acclaimed debut CD *Listen Love* has been hailed as an outstanding new release, marking the debut of an important new jazz singer, who 'delivers powerful versions of non-standards in a crystal-clear voice with diamond-cut phrasing' (*The Philadelphia Inquirer*).

In *Anything I Can Do . . . You Can Do Better*, she shares her own story of how she struggled to become first a journalist, then a singer, as well as the stories of those who, like her, have followed their creative dreams, offering practical insights so that you too can change your life.

Anything I Can Do . . . You Can Do Better

How to unlock
your creative dreams and
change your life

Tessa Souter

Vermilion
LONDON

1 3 5 7 9 10 8 6 4 2

First published in 2006 by Vermilion,
an imprint of Ebury Publishing, Random House,
20 Vauxhall Bridge Road, London SW1V 2SA

Random House Australia (Pty) Limited
20 Alfred Street, Milsons Point, Sydney,
New South Wales 2061, Australia

Random House New Zealand Limited
18 Poland Road, Glenfield,
Auckland 10, New Zealand

Random House South Africa (Pty) Limited
Isle of Houghton, Corner of Boundary Road & Carse O'Gowrie,
Houghton 2198, South Africa

The Random House Group Limited Reg. No. 954009

Papers used by Vermilion are natural, recyclable products
made from wood grown in sustainable forests.

Typeset by SX Composing DTP, Rayleigh, Essex
Printed and bound in Great Britain by Mackays of Chatham plc, Kent

A CIP catalogue record for this book
is available from the British Library

ISBN 0-09190256-8

To You

This sickness to create. What is it?
Jean Cocteau

Contents

Introduction

You *shall* go to the ball!
The Good Fairy to Cinderella

Since I decided to actively pursue my dream to be a singer, I have never been so happy – or so miserable. It's not so much an emotional roller coaster ride as like being picked up in the hands of a huge giant, carried around for a brief period of respite, and then dashed to the ground. Over and over again. A few months (or *years*) of that will turn anyone into a bloody pulp, which means you need guts to spare. So the first thing you should truly understand and acknowledge about following a creative dream is that – contrary to what you might imagine – it's not all elation and joy, it *hurts*: even when you 'make it'. Why else would so many rock gods and movie stars implode once they get there.

Yes, there are a lucky few, who are born or married to the rich and famous, or who are well-connected, or both. But even they have to prove themselves. Think of Sofia Coppola's ten-year transition from critically panned actress in her father's *The Godfather Part III* to Oscar-nominated director and Oscar-winning screenwriter for *Lost In Translation*. I think it is safe to say that *no* singer was discovered by someone who overheard them singing in the shower. *No* writer was discovered by a literary agent accidentally coming across their private journal hidden under the bed. Paul Auster sent his first manuscript to nineteen publishers or more before one of them picked it up and made it into a best seller. My voice has been described as:

'The most deeply and profoundly moving voice I have heard in the past ten years!' by one major label. Another major label said: 'I don't hear anything special in her voice.' Both were talking about the *exact same* demo CD.

A recent article in the *New York Times* (24 April, 2004), 'Going Early Into That Good Night', announced the findings of a new study ('The Cost of the Muse: Poets Die Young') that investigated the age at death of prominent writers around the world. The study, conducted at the Learning Research Institute at California State University, San Bernadino, shows that poets tend to die younger than other writers. Poets had an average life span of 66.2 years, compared with 72.7 for non-fiction writers and 68.9 for novelists. According to a separate study, musicians fare even less well, with an average life span of only 57.2 years. The study showed that roughly 20 per cent of eminent poets had committed suicide, compared with a suicide rate of 1 per cent in the general population.

There's a reason so many great artists commit suicide. It isn't only that they are 'sensitive' souls – although that doesn't help. The hard fact is, if you're chasing a dream, it takes over your life. It becomes an obsession. And it tests you continually. No matter how brilliant you are, you are going to lose confidence, you are going to face rejection. As many people will want to pull you down as lift you up. It takes supreme faith – in your ability, in the universe, in God, in whatever it takes – to keep you going. Once you reach the point of no return, you will not even know why you are continuing, but you won't be able to help it. 'I am working,' wrote Frida Kahlo to a friend. 'But even that, I don't know how or why.'

You will be a fish on a hook; an addict with a habit. You will be broke. You will be in debt (unless you are lucky enough to be a trust fund baby). You will wonder if there was ever a time when your friends were merely friends, as opposed to full-time cheerleaders (my friend Vern calls it 'diva-sitting' when I get so low my friends have to come over and hold my hand). You will call your closest friends in tears at 5 a.m. You will feel guilty about that BUT YOU WON'T BE ABLE TO HELP YOURSELF. And it is exhausting, for you and everyone around you.

When I was a child, a male friend of my mother's was in love with a famous singer. She was constantly on the phone to him in tears, saying what a bad singer she was, how awful she looked, how she was a failure. We didn't know what she was *talking* about. She was beautiful and successful. She was on *Top of the Pops,* Britain's most popular TV music show, for heaven's sake. Her insecurities didn't make sense to us. *Then.* Now I understand. I too have been to the edge of reason. What am I saying? I have fallen *off* the edge; like Coyote, whistling to the bottom of the ravine and exploding quietly at the bottom . . . Poof!

You are going to have to prove yourself to yourself, your family, your friends, the world, the *universe*; prove your staying power, prove you're worth it, prove your belief in yourself. And you are going to have to do it over and over (and *over*) again. There's a long list of people who didn't stay the course: Judy Garland, Vincent Van Gogh, Diane Arbus, Virginia Woolf, Spalding Gray, Susannah McCorkle, Sylvia Plath, Anne Sexton . . . all killed themselves. Many others drank themselves to death. Or died of the effects of drug abuse. Because pursuing your dream is such a painful endeavour a significant percentage of people can't do it without medicating themselves, even if nowadays that means anti-depressants (the modern artist's laudanum).

At a particularly stressful period in my life, down to the wire (I mean, bare, *fizzing* wire, with sparks flying off it), scrabbling to get the money to send out press kits and demos in an effort to get somewhere, fending off creditors (afraid to open my mail, screening my phone calls), doing everything myself (designing and making my own brochures, postcards, clothes), literally losing my hair, I went to stay with a friend to 'rest'. As soon as I arrived I had to be restrained from running to the computer to work on my latest brochure design. All evening I felt like Ulysses, lashed to the mast, resisting the siren call of the computer screen flickering in my peripheral vision. And my hosts told me the next day that they could hear me in the next room whimpering in my sleep all night.

There were days when things were so bad that I couldn't *even* worry. After my sold-out debut at London's Pizza Express, Dean Street (Good Giant carrying me around in big, comforting hands) I returned to New York to an eviction notice from my landlord for being two months late with the rent (giant dashing me to the ground again). There was no *point* fretting over it. There was nothing I could do about it anyway. At those times I would just have to breathe; literally just concentrate on my breath coming in and out of my body, because that was the only thing I *could* do. No, you won't know why you are continuing. The only thing you will know is that you can't *not* continue. 'Even when you're a cripple you carry on painting,' said John Lennon in 1970, referring to the creative drive. 'I would paint if I couldn't move!'

You will struggle with money, relationships, envy (other people's and – even worse! – your *own*!) self-confidence, ego, faith in yourself, in God, in your very soul. Pianist Keith Jarrett put it brilliantly in *The Man and His Music*, talking about one of his albums. '*Spirit* was born of drowning in a certain place so I could come up to the surface in another – without forgetting the drowning and without dying.'

Still want to do it? Okay then. Because, in spite of everything, I can safely say that just pursuing my dream – let alone achieving it – has been the best thing that I have ever given myself. I hope that this book will be your good giant that will catch you before you fall. But most of all I hope it helps you realise that (as my agent Rebecca kept saying to me over and over again when I was writing this book), 'You *can* do it, Tessa. I believe in you, and I *know* you can do this.'

This book is dedicated to you.

Chapter 1:
All You Have To Do Is Dream:
Getting Started

All glory comes from daring to begin.

Eugene F. Ware

Congratulations. You've bought this book, or are loved and believed in enough to have had it given to you by a friend or family member who's up to here with you wasting your talent and/or railing against (or comparing yourself unfavourably to) all those who *are* brave enough to be doing what you wish *you* dared to do. And now you're ready to get serious about pursuing your creative dream. This chapter is about *how* to do that – specifically, how to begin.

Now, some of you reading this book may have had trouble making a start because you're afraid to commit yourself to the wrong path. 'What if I change my mind and realise I should have been a painter instead of a poet?' Or you aren't entirely sure you really *want* your creative dream. 'Who wants to deal with the paparazzi, right?' When a record label first expressed interest in me, at the same time as a radio station wanted to do a story on me, I called my best friend, Neil, in a complete panic about how to cope with the attention. He brought me back down to earth by saying drily: '*I dunno. Why don't you ask Madonna?*'

Or, maybe your dream is *such* a burning desire that you're afraid it will take over your life (it will, by the way). Maybe you fear success, or failure – or both. Perhaps you're afraid of being 'better' than your parents. Or, of making your friends jealous. Or, of looking foolish in front of people by falling flat on your face. Maybe your dream doesn't feel 'realistic'. 'It'll never happen,' you sigh. Well, no, it won't. Not if you're waiting for inspiration, blobbed out on your couch, eating chocs and watching *Oprah* re-runs.

I've been there. And no-one knows more than I do that there's nothing more daunting than making a start – whether it's going to the gym, cleaning your house or writing a novel. Which is why the universe invented procrastination. Renee Knight, a BBC documentary film maker turned scriptwriter, got addicted to playing backgammon on her computer when she first switched to writing. But at least it got her in front of the computer. Former scriptwriter (*The Archers*, *Boon*, *Heartbeat* and *Doctors)* turned best-selling author (*Honeycote*, *Making Hay*, *Wild Oats* and *An Eligible Bachelor*), Veronica Henry claims to have 'the cleanest lav in the Midlands!' referring to her favourite procrastination tool (also one of mine) – cleaning. 'When it all slots into place, and the words start to spill, that is when writing is a pleasure,' she says. 'But there are times when anything would be more pleasurable than booting up the laptop to look at the turgid drivel you churned out the day before.'

Sometimes I would use procrastinating about one thing (calling musicians for a particular gig) to stop procrastinating about another thing (writing). But, believe me, once you've actually made a *start*, you'll find it easier than you think. American author Anne Lamott wrote a wonderful book on how to be a writer, the title of which (*Bird By Bird*) came from a story she tells in the book about a bird project her brother had to write for school. He kept putting it off until finally, the day before he was due to hand it in, he still hadn't written a word and was tearing his hair out. Their father sat him down and said: 'Just take it bird by bird, son. Bird by bird.' Excellent advice. And it works. Because the short answer to how to get anywhere in *anything*, is you *start* and then you just don't stop.

'If writing is your dream, then write. Whatever. It drives me crazy when people say "I want to write." What's stopping them?' says novelist Veronica Henry. 'Just do it. Everyone in the world is entitled to be a writer – there's no entrance exam. Anyone who puts pen to paper can call themselves a writer, in my view. But you do have to write!' If that sounds harsh, it's only because she knows what she's talking about, having been through the doubts and fears herself. 'I didn't get round to writing what I wanted to write for years. I was a television script editor, then a script writer for fifteen years before it finally dawned on me that I really yearned to write commercial women's fiction. I did the classic, irritating, wannabe thing of picking up books and saying "I could write this". And after years of bleating about it, my husband and TV agent each turned round to me and said, out of sheer frustration, "Then do it!" Rather shocked by their vehemence, I eventually did.'

Of course, this is easier said than done. A conversation with a friend, a kind word from a teacher, some positive feedback, listening to an amazing piece of music, a visit to a museum, reading an incredible novel, or a good self-help book – any of these might make you cry out: 'Yes! Yes! I *want* to and I *can*!' But it is my sad duty to warn you that however inspired you feel when you start off, you *won't* feel like that all the time. At other times you will think – as did Virginia Woolf, Brahms, Van Gogh, among countless other great artists – words to the effect of *who the hell do I think I am?* Inspiration and hopelessness are as married to each other (and about as happily) as Liz Taylor and Richard Burton in *Who's Afraid of Virginia Woolf*.

By now everyone knows the Goethe quote: 'Whatever you think you can do or believe you can, begin it. Action has magic, grace and power in it.' But it's not *quite* that simple. Because, although starting is important (duh!), at no point are you more vulnerable to stopping dead in your tracks than at the beginning. As Martha Graham once said: 'The ordeal of isolation, the ordeal of loneliness, the ordeal of doubt, the ordeal of vulnerability which it takes to compose in any medium is hard to face.' It's no wonder so many of us give up before we even begin.

Have you ever heard of Charlotte Brontë's novel *Emma*? No? Ah. That will be because when she showed the first few pages to her new husband (she married late – thank goodness!), he said: 'Hmm. Not up to your usual standard, dearest . . .' And she never wrote another word, of that, or any other novel, ever again. So the first thing I used to do, when young journalists would ask my advice about how to get into journalism, was show them my enormous file of rejection letters and tell them to keep believing in themselves.

When I first started out pitching ideas to magazines, I'd assume that any rejections were because the idea was bad. 'Oh, how could I have pitched such an appalling idea? I'm an idiot! I'm so embarrassed!' I'd rail against myself, praying that I never bumped into that editor anywhere. Then two or three months later I'd see the exact same idea in another magazine, proving that it wasn't the idea that was wrong, after all. Occasionally my ideas were even *stolen*. One time, an editor of a major newspaper held me off for six weeks, saying (week after week) he loved the idea and to please call him back next week. And then he published a book excerpt on the exact same subject by a famous war photographer, thus precluding the possibility of my selling the idea to a rival newspaper.

I could have railed against my bad luck. How hard it was to break in as an unknown. Oh, all right, I admit it, I *did*. But, as my friend Mansur likes to say: 'There are no failures and mistakes, only lessons'. After a few of these, er, lessons, I finally got it that yes I *was* hooked into the *zeitgeist* of magazine journalism, and if I got a rejection from one magazine I'd better not just sit on my couch and suck down another pint of ice cream while I swooned over Commander Ryker on *Star Trek: The Next Generation*, I'd better send the idea off to another magazine *right now*! Ultimately, these so-called setbacks were what inspired me to learn how to present my ideas (and myself as the writer to write them) more convincingly.

So start. And don't bash yourself up for not being able to play like Rachmaninoff right away – which is what happened to my own piano playing *when I was eleven years old*. 'Remember, your artist is a child,' writes Julia Cameron in her essential *The Artist's Way*. 'The artist child must begin by crawling. Baby steps will follow and there will be falls – yecchy first paintings, beginning films that look like unedited home movies, first poems that would shame a greeting card . . . In recovering from our creative blocks, it is necessary to go gently and slowly . . . No high jumping, please! Mistakes are necessary! Stumbles are normal. Progress, not perfection, is what we should be asking of ourselves.'

HOT TIP
Dare to dream. And don't let anything or anyone – especially yourself – put a cap on it. Revel in it, embellish it, write it down, visualise it (in glorious Technicolor), hone that dream until you know exactly what you want.

IF YOU DON'T HAVE A DREAM . . .

Take the first step in faith. You don't have to see the whole
staircase, just take the first step.

Dr. Martin Luther King Jr.

Ever since I was a child I imagined I would grow up to be a
singer. I loved writing stories, too. But singing was something
else. I just did it as naturally as speaking. In fact, it wasn't
something I just did; it was something I *was*. From the age of
about six, I used to wake up singing every morning, and my
brother and I spent hours together composing songs and lyrics
and taping them on our parents' reel-to-reel tape recorder. At
fourteen, I played guitar for all my friends at school during the
lunch break and everyone agreed that to be a singer was my
destiny. But I took another path first.

I got married at sixteen and became a single parent at
eighteen, intermittently going back to school to get my O and A
levels, before going to university to study English Literature. I
was good at writing and, although I sang all the time, the idea of
doing it professionally seemed like a dream that would never
come true. Instead, at twenty-nine, I got my first full-time job
editing reports and proposals for building projects. Good
practice for working with words. But mental torture. So, determined to work on magazines, I got the *Guardian* newspaper
every Monday (when Creative and Media jobs are advertised)
and I applied for *at least* two jobs a week, even if there weren't
any suitable ones. It was good practice in writing application
letters, which I eventually honed to perfection.

Sometimes I'd get an interview. Sometimes I'd never hear back.
But eventually *Parents* magazine called me in (out of one hundred
applicants) and, miraculously, I got the job. Within a year I had
graduated from editorial assistant to writer and chief sub-editor,

assisted on fashion and news and had learned the basics of the magazine business. As for writing, I have to thank the editor, who one day announced in a meeting (to my utter horror, and surprise) that I would be writing an article on introducing children to 'grown-up' activities, like the opera and ballet.

What? I had never written anything for a magazine in my life. Terrified, I called my writer friend Sarah Litvinoff, author of *The Confidence Plan: Essential Steps to a New You*, who at the time I barely knew, and asked if I could read her the first paragraph over the phone. 'Of course!' she said. When I'd finished she said: 'Oh, it's wonderful! I can't *wait* to hear the next paragraph!' Eventually, paragraph by paragraph (all read to Sarah over the phone) I finished it. The editor loved it and – boom! – I was away! To the extent that, a year later, I left in order to do freelance sub-editing on bigger magazines, where I earned more money and broadened my knowledge of the magazine industry. The freelance writer bit came later.

But all the while I still harboured my secret desire to sing. I sang for my friends and family. I sang in the shower. And when I moved to America, where I supported myself as a house cleaner to survive while I established myself as a freelance writer, I spent many hours on my hands and knees scrubbing floors, singing at the top of my voice and fantasising about one day performing in public.

The constant singing kept my voice in shape. But, just as importantly, it kept the dream alive. It was like a seed that I kept warm and fed constantly with dreams and mental pictures of myself singing to vast crowds, engaging the audience with witty repartee – never mind that when I actually did start singing in public (to . . . er, *small* crowds) I couldn't even open my eyes I was so terrified.

START AT THE VERY BEGINNING

You can't wait for inspiration. You have to go after it with a club.

Jack London

To manifest a dream, it helps to start out with a specific goal. You can always change your mind later. So you want to be a writer? Do you want to write novels, short stories, articles, essays, non-fiction, a memoir? An actor. Do you want to act on the stage? In movies? In both? When I decided to make my career change from writer to singer I enlisted the help of one of Britain's foremost life coaches, Mark Forster, author of *Get Everything Done and Still Have Time To Play* and *How To Make Your Dreams Come True,* whose first piece of homework was for me to write out my Five-Year Plan. Writing it out really helped me identify *exactly* what I wanted. So go to it. Make an appointment with yourself to set aside an hour or so to write *your* Five-Year Plan. And have fun with it. It's a dream – for now. No pressure. Don't get caught up in 'that could never happen'. Play around. Swim in it. Make the dream as 'unrealistic' as you like. In fact, forget 'realistic'. That's just a word other people (or *you*) use to rain on your parade.

HOT TIP
It's a good idea to have a five-year plan, a three-year plan, and a one-year plan, because knowing where you want to go is the first step in actually getting there one day. If you need to, get a more know-ledgeable friend to help you come up with one. Or research the career trajectory of someone you admire to gauge what is realistic, bearing in mind wild cards such as pure dumb luck.

It's actually amazing what can be done when you decide what you want and really go for it. Imagine someone saying: 'I've always wanted to be a writer. My friends love my letters!' How many times have you (and I) dismissed in your mind (if not out loud) someone who has said that to you? But that's what inspired *me* to become a writer. And how about: 'I've always dreamed of being a professional singer! So what that I'm nearly forty-three! My boyfriend/mother/best friend/*other biased source* says I sound great in the shower!' Ridiculous, right? Yet, here I am. And as you read on you will get to know several other creative people (who have generously shared their stories throughout these pages in order that you might benefit from their examples) who have also made their dreams come true.

Before novelist Karen Quinn, author of best seller *The Ivy Chronicles*, started writing, she had always made her living doing practical work of some kind. 'First I was a lawyer, then I worked for American Express doing advertising, then I owned a small educational consulting business helping families get their children into New York City's best schools.' She was also painting as a hobby. 'I quit my educational consulting business because I wasn't making enough money at it (my ex-partner still runs the business today) and for the first time, I found myself unemployed and not sure what to do,' she says. But she had always secretly longed to write a novel. 'I had all these amazing stories to tell from my years working with New York families and their children. My husband wanted me to get a job, but I told him that I wanted to write a best seller (yes, I aimed for the stars) about my time as a private-school admissions consultant.'

As soon as she began to write, she fell in love with it. 'I looked forward to waking up every morning to create another ten pages of my story. Writing *The Ivy Chronicles* was the most amazing and fulfilling professional experience I've ever had. The book is the story of a woman who is fired from a big corporate job and who reinvents herself by starting a company helping parents get their kids into the best schools. Writing the tale was a cathartic experience.' Karen's story is a wonderful example of the importance of not capping your dreams. She wanted to write a best seller, and she did.

Interior designer Susan Cozzi hasn't been so lucky as to follow her childhood artistic dream – yet. 'My original talent was dance. That is what I was put here on this earth to do. And I knew it from the moment I can remember my consciousness as a child,' she says. 'With zero encouragement, I started dancing late as a child. However, with *continued* zero encouragement, despite winning a dance scholarship to NYU, I gave up and stopped pursuing my dream.' Susan was encouraged to follow in the steps of her older sister to study art. And though talented in art too, she says, 'that extra life-fulfilling passion wasn't there the way it was for dance.' After two years, she switched, not to dance, but to studying literature, which was more in line with her own interests at the time than art.

After twelve progressively challenging, rewarding, and successful years in book publishing, Susan was faced, at thirty-five, with no job. 'During the five months that I didn't work, and half-heartedly searched out publishing positions, I embarked on a soul-destroying internal search of why I had given up on my dream to dance,' she says. My life had been a nagging unfulfilled question because it wasn't a life of dance. If I had quickly got another job, I never would have taken the time that my identifying self needed. But at the end of my soul searching, I decided that at least I would give my second-best talent a second shot even though I had less confidence in myself in art than in dance.'

She signed up for an interior design class at her local college, and enrolled fully the following semester. 'When I told my mother that I was going back to school to change careers, she said, "What are you doing that for? Can't you just get another job?" It was enough to almost completely pull the rug out from underneath me all over again,' says Susan, who still feels angry with her parents at the lack of encouragement she received with her dance. Determined to throw herself into her chosen career this time around, she started looking for work after only one full-time semester. 'I decided to get right on the boat, get a job in my new field and attend school part time. How'd I do it? I went to one of the world's most renowned Italian furniture manufacturers, walked into the showroom, and asked, "How do I get a job here?" And the gods were on my side because there was a job opening. I began a week later.' After that it was a question of just keeping going.

I'd love to know what would have happened if Susan had put that same determination into getting back in to dance. But at least she knew what her dream was. Some people are so removed from believing they can have their dream they don't even know what it is. When I co-life coached Clare – my recently-made-redundant friend – we took it in turns once a week to identify our goals and work towards them. She often complained that I was lucky to know what I wanted to do (sing) and that she had no idea what she wanted to do with her life. Then one day she confided in me her childhood dream to be an artist. Her first step, we decided, was simply to go to an art supplies store and buy crayons, paper and pastels. Soon she was drawing every day, and within six months she'd moved to Europe, where she set herself up in an artist friend's studio. Amazingly, she was exhibiting in group shows before the year was out.

As it happens, she fell off the wagon when she became involved with a discouraging boyfriend. Perhaps she manifested the boyfriend because deep down she was afraid to pursue an artist's life. Or perhaps – like Susan – she gave in to her father's internalised protestations about how she should live her life according to his dreams – in this case to 'do something sensible'. Watch out for the things you might be doing to self-sabotage, particularly at the beginning. It *is* scary to stick your neck out – especially to be judged by something so arbitrary as other people's tastes – but no-one can make you believe that your dreams can't come true, unless you let them. So don't be your own worst enemy. Stay away from naysayers and make an effort to surround yourself with encouraging, inspiring people instead (for more on this subject, see Chapter Five: Love Me or Leave Me).

Because, up *until* Clare became discouraged by her boyfriend, she'd been working towards everything she'd ever dreamed of as a child. And with some success. She had an exhibition, a studio, friends were buying her paintings. It was beyond anything she could have imagined possible, especially in such a short time. Proof that, to quote Patanjali (circa first to third century BC): 'When you are inspired by some great purpose, some extraordinary project, all your thoughts break their bonds; your mind transcends limitations, your consciousness expands in every direction, and you find yourself in a new, great and wonderful world. Dormant forces, faculties and talents become alive and you discover yourself to be a greater person by far than you ever dreamed yourself to be.'

So dream big – the bigger the better! And never let anything (youth, age, gender, race, so-called 'failures' and setbacks) or any*one* (parents, teachers, friends, lovers, family, employers and especially yourself) put a cap on your dreams. You will feel better for trying and 'failing' than if you never try at all. Rudyard Kipling didn't let it stop him when, at the beginning of his career, the editor of the *San Francisco Examiner* declined to accept any more of his work, saying: 'I'm sorry, Mr Kipling. But you just don't know how to use the English language. This isn't a kindergarten for amateur writers.'

YOU *SHALL* GO TO THE BALL

Defeat is not the worst of failures.
Not to have tried is the true failure.
George E. Woodberry

When James Browne decided he wanted to work in the music industry he started out as the night-time elevator operator at a local radio station in New York. 'I had no credibility at all. People would ring the bell at 2 a.m. and I would go down and get them.' But he got to know everyone on the late shift and, since there was plenty of spare time between people coming in, he got to hang out in the studio and learn something about the mechanics of DJ-ing. 'If I'd just walked in off the street I wouldn't have had that experience,' he says. When someone wasn't able to come in one night, he was able to fill in, and eventually he got given a shot at the midnight to 4 a.m. slot. Unpaid. Within a year he had become the station's music director and then a successful producer. 'Like my grandfather used to say: "Everything is possible if you just show up for work,"' says James.

Working for free (as an intern), or for little pay, is an excellent way in to a chosen profession. It gets you close to the subject and into a good position to learn the business, as well as giving you the opportunity of being in the right place at the right time when an entry level job comes up. Film director Nic Roeg started out at seventeen as a gofer at a film production company. Comedian and TV show host (Discovery Channel's dating show, *Perfect Partner*) Daphne Brogden got her start by interning at various TV and radio stations (see Chapter Three: I Will Survive). Countless journalists got their start interning on a magazine. Many singers started their careers as backing vocalists.

HOT TIP

Get as close as possible to your chosen profession, even if that means volunteering. Now a successful DJ and presenter, and author of *The Quotable Musician*, Sheila Anderson started out on the radio as a volunteer. One day she asked one of the DJs if he would train her and he agreed. Her vibrant personality and intelligence got her noticed. And, of course, she was on the spot when a paid job came up.

As for me, with a lot of encouragement (okay, bullying), I started taking my dream to sing more seriously after I went to my first open mic session and *sang*. It was a combination of wanting to please my boyfriend at the time, Mark, my own unconscious yearning to do it, and being a journalist, that led me back to my childhood dream. I had written an article about life coaches in *The Times* and, through that, I'd met life coach, and author of several inspirational books, Laura Berman Fortgang, who became my life coach for three months. She started out gently: 'What do you want to focus on during our time together?' 'I think singing,' I said, innocently, 'because that's something I've wanted to do all my life.' I say 'innocently' because from the moment I told her that my first step should probably be to go to an open mic, she called me on why I hadn't gone to one yet at every one of our sessions until I did. 'You don't have to sing if you don't want to,' she said. 'Just go.'

So I went, and I sang, and I really enjoyed it. Then I went back. Then I went back again. And again. Soon I was going every week. But everything that has happened in my career since then *started* at the moment I stood up in front of that roomful of strangers and sang. People were encouraging and asked where they could hear me perform and I gradually built up my confidence and graduated to singing at jazz jam sessions. About a year later I sat in on a friend's gig and the club owner liked and hired me too. Looking over the notes I wrote about that very first time I see that my heart felt like it was going to burst out of my chest at the very thought of singing in public, I was so terrified. But, as Susan Jeffers says in her must-read, *Feel the Fear And Do It Anyway*, 'The only way to get over a fear of doing something is to go out . . . and do it!'

Once you actually make a start you will find that the universe will join in and help you. 'Concerning all acts of initiative there is one elementary truth . . . that the moment one definitely commits oneself, then Providence moves too. All sorts of things occur to help one that would otherwise never have occurred,' wrote W.H. Murray. And that has been my experience whenever I have actively pursued something. All sorts of unexpected events and people have appeared in my life to keep me going in my various endeavours – from my wonderful accountant, Olen, in San Francisco, to the friends there who helped me in my quest to be a journalist. They loaned me a computer for three years, let me send international faxes and refused to let me pay for them, introduced me to all their friends as 'Tessa the talented writer' (as opposed to 'Tessa the charwoman') until, after about two years, I 'made it': i.e., I was earning enough as a writer to be able to stop cleaning houses.

Josh Kornbluth, a monologist and screenwriter, started when his friend Scott encouraged him to get up and riff at a comedy open mic. He was scared to death – even though bolstered by his friend's belief in him – but he got up anyway. That is, he *started*. People *other than Scott* laughed. And from that moment on he was on his way. Now, several successful monologues and one well-reviewed movie later, he is what he always wanted to be – a comedian. Married comedy team Steve Epstein and Naima Hassan (AKA The Black and the Jew) also tested the waters at an open mic the first time they performed. 'By the time we went up, there were four Japanese businessmen in the place who didn't speak English.' But they'd started. Now they perform to packed houses around New York where they have developed a cult following.

Actor Graham McTavish got hooked on acting at university. One of the most motivated people I know (he wrote an entire novel when he was twelve), straight out of college he toured the country with his own one-man production of Samuel Beckett's *Krapp's Last Tape*. A few years later, with his friend, Nick Pace (then a struggling actor, later a successful artist, by the way), he co-wrote a two-man show about Vincent Van Gogh and his brother, Theo, called *Letters From the Yellow Chair*. They took it all over the world, performing in theatres and major art galleries – from the UK to the US, Australia, even Hawaii.

Lyricist Bruce Heckman began when he composed a song to be sung at his son's wedding. 'Hearing it being performed by a professional band, I was struck dumb,' he says. 'I have continued to write, and recorded a CD of *Jazz Psalms* with music by Loren Stillman that was sung by Kate McGarry.' It was the fulfilment of a childhood dream. 'When I was nine years old I wrote a very short story about myself and my two younger brothers. My aunt gave me fifty cents and I thought (deep in my undeveloped commercial recesses) that this would be a lucrative profession when I grew up,' says Bruce. 'So a life of writing poems and stories began that was rewarded with a few prizes and five dollars for my first published poem.'

Carol Hall, who wrote the score for *The Best Little Whorehouse in Texas*, started out as a student writing tunes for college shows. 'It wasn't professional, but it gave me the idea that it was really fun to stand in the back and hear people laughing at something I had written.' But she really got going when she had what she now calls 'the audacity' to call the singer Mabel Mercer and offer her a song.

Mercer (see Chapter Ten: Up, Up And Away) was a New York institution whose weekly performances were attended by all the singing stars (including Frank Sinatra and Barbra Streisand).

'She did songs that no-one did, that no-one had heard, so I thought it would be a good idea to call her up and tell her she needed to hear my songs,' says Carol. Even more audacious, when she didn't hear back after a few days, she called her again. 'Miss Mercer. About those songs?' she said. Mercer chose two, including 'Jenny Rebecca' which Streisand then heard her sing, and subsequently recorded herself. 'It was a great start because it meant that I could call people up and impress them with: "Two of my songs are being done by Mabel Mercer."' Let alone later being able to name-drop Streisand.

When Jane Lyle, picture researcher turned best-selling author of *The Lover's Tarot*, *The Destiny Cup* and *Sacred Sexuality*, came up with the idea for her first book, *Understanding Body Language*, in 1993, she exhibited a similar *chutzpah*. 'I just found out relevant names in the publishing company and posted it off with a prayer!' she explains. 'It helped that a friend of a friend knew a company who was looking for someone to write about body language. And it wasn't a proper "deal", just a fee,' she says. 'However, it was worth it just to get published and have a book to talk about to other publishers.' It always helps to have work to show, even articles. Clearly, they need to know you can actually produce a sustained body of work as well as write. They are taking a financial risk after all.

Showing confidence, even if it's born of ignorance, is a good thing. But keep it within reason. Don't do what an actor I know did at a theatre audition for the play *Robin Hood*. When he turned up he found out that the director was in the loo, so he went and knocked on the stall door. When the surprised director asked who it was, he replied in a booming God voice: 'Robin Hood!' Needless to say he didn't get the part.

Photographer Michael Becker had been a successful musician and producer in Los Angeles when his father became terminally ill and he moved across country to take care of him. During those six months he started taking photographs just to relax. 'Then I started shooting friends' publicity shots for them. Then I did a CD cover. And gradually I started thinking, as soon as I'm good enough I should start charging for it.' Three years later he has evolved his own very distinctive painterly style of landscape and portrait photography.

But it began when a friend he was chatting to mentioned wanting an old Rolleiflex camera. Michael had one that his grandfather had given him. 'I thought of it as almost an ornament back then,' he says. 'I hadn't put a roll of film in it for fifteen years. So I thought let's see if it still works, and lo and behold, it did. And then the obsession took over.' He started poking around on the Internet asking questions to learn more ('Everything from technical stuff to how do you learn to do exposure like Ansel Adams did') and before he knew it, photography began to take over from his music career. Once he started taking pictures photography work came his way. 'My girlfriend [now wife], who was producing some reality shows for ABC, found out they needed someone to shoot promo photos. I did one job for them and they kept hiring me,' he says. 'It was a really lucky break.'

Well, yes, it was. In a world where so many people are vying for so few spots, luck has to be a part of whether you succeed or not. When Napoleon was choosing generals, having ascertained whether or not he was a good soldier, he would ask: 'Yes, but is he lucky?' Then again, if Michael hadn't been taking photographs in the first place; if he hadn't made it his business to learn all the technical stuff; if he hadn't decided (at forty, mind you) to do something completely new; in other words if he hadn't *started*, no amount of luck in the world would have got him that job. The point is, your beginnings don't need to be huge. They just need to be one step in the direction of where you want to end up.

How you can do it, too

1. Dare to dream and *believe* in your dream. Did the stars of the tiny independent movie *Sideways* dream that it would get so many Oscar nominations? Probably. Whether they thought the dream would come true is another matter. But for all those people who *didn't* think *Sideways* would get to the Oscars (and I'm sure there were many), its success is proof that obscurity, tiny budgets, middle age and geeky looks are no barrier to success.

2. Having identified your dream, identify how to make a start. If you are an aspiring novelist, write. Do it every day, even if it's just for an hour. If you want to be a singer, find an open mic or even a karaoke bar and sing. If you want to be a freelance journalist, research the publications you want to write for and send them ideas that fit in with their style. If you want to paint, paint. If you want to be an actor, join a class and get into amateur productions. If you want to be a stand-up comic, go to an open mic session, get up there, and do your thing. If you want to dance, go to dance classes. You've got the picture. To quote the Nike ad – just *do* it.

3. Study. Study. Study. Know your subject. There are a million books that give practical tips on how to write journalistic pitch letters, how to negotiate the music industry, how to draw. And there is a great teacher or course out there for your chosen subject. Decide whether going back to school would be worth it for you in terms of time and money. Some fields (jazz, for example) might be better studied 'on the job'. Ask around and then go with your gut feeling.

4.   Surround yourself as much as possible with people who are doing what you are doing. Find a mentor (see Chapter Six: Help! I Need Somebody). Get to know someone who has been working in your field for some time and is happy to help you negotiate the 'what to' and 'what *not* to'. I nominated a wonderful writer I admired called Martin Plimmer as a mini-mentor when I was struggling to be a freelance writer and he answered endless questions on the phone about how to pitch an idea and who to pitch it to. In music, studying for four years with my mentor, vocal jazz legend Mark Murphy, was like putting on seven league boots.

5.   Start at the top. Don't be afraid to be 'cheeky'. When I first started approaching magazines with ideas, I would go to the lowest person on the masthead. It didn't produce any results. However, once I started approaching people at the very top I had more success. A top editor is more likely to know what they want. Plus, if they like your pitch and pass it down the line, it looks like the instructions came from above. Similarly, start with the big magazines. Why confine yourself from the beginning? I unsuccessfully pitched a story on advertising and the tobacco industry to every obscure magazine in London, but it was the editor of *Elle,* Maggie Alderson (now reinvented as a successful novelist in Australia), who had the guts to commission it.

6.   Use procrastinating about one thing to help you get on with another thing. When I'd be juggling writing jobs, I found it much easier to make a start on the least daunting of them. The ease with which I'd be able to write that one would then usually inspire me to continue with the others.

7.   Take it 'bird by bird'. If you need to do a specific task that you've been putting off, make it as small as possible by not imagining the big picture. For example, when I felt daunted about writing this book I found the best way to start

working was not to think: 'I must finish this *entire book*!' Much more effective was say to myself, 'Oh, I'll just read what I've done so far.' Then, when it was right in front of me I'd find I couldn't resist writing.

8.   Don't give up before you even begin. Treat failures and setbacks as lessons, and soldier on. To quote Rudyard Kipling, if you can take a risk and lose everything and then be brave enough to start again from the beginning, ' . . . yours is the Earth and everything that's in it . . .'

The refusal to rest content, the willingness to risk excess on behalf of one's obsessions, is what distinguishes artists from entertainers, and what makes some artists adventurers on behalf of us all.
John Updike

Chapter Two:
Walk This Way:
What To Do And How To Do It

I remember once hearing one of my younger brothers telling his
girlfriend my story, what my career was like – I was born, I was
talented, I got into piano, I had this neat place and I worked with
Miles Davis. He left out this giant part which was the struggle!

Keith Jarrett, jazz pianist

So you've accepted the 'calling' to be a painter/singer/circus
clown/comedian/pianist/whatever. And you've actually made a
start. You've been getting up early and putting in two solid
hours on your novel every morning. You have joined the
community of singers at your nearest open mic. You're hanging
out at a local musicians' jam. You've performed at a comedy
club and people (at least your drunken friends) laughed. You've
found a studio and are painting every day. Whichever step
you've taken it's been enough to convince you that you want to
go all the way. But how?

In this chapter I want to help you to define the all-important
practical principles of exactly *what* to do to turn your dream
into a reality. Because as Keith Jarrett points out in the quote
that opens this chapter, there are a few stages to go through
between being born and getting to play with Miles Davis.

HOLD MY HAND AND I'LL TAKE YOU THERE

All our dreams can come true,
if we have the courage to pursue them.
Walt Disney

When I was thinking about buying a computer from a catalogue recently, the girl who was helping me over the phone asked me all the standard questions, including: 'What do you use a computer for?' I told her I was writing a book and wrote freelance magazine articles, and that I was also a singer and used Adobe Photoshop to design my brochures and postcards. 'Oh I've always wanted to be a journalist!' she exclaimed. 'I just don't know where to start. Can you advise me?' She was smart. She saw an opportunity (to talk to a real working journalist) and she grabbed it. Over the next hour on the phone, I realised, in telling her what I knew, that (miraculously and unexpectedly) I *did* know where to start. And, not only that, but that there were very specific actions she could take. I hadn't really thought about exactly how I'd broken into journalism myself until she asked. At the end of the call she went off with a list of things to do, people to approach and the beginnings of a plan.

I also put her in touch with a journalist I serendipitously happened to know in her area. I suggested that she find part-time work (even unpaid) as an intern, either for a busy local journalist or on a magazine. I told her to read all her favourite publications from cover to cover for about three months until she felt sure of the kind of story they were looking for, and then to pitch her idea to the editor (whose name she should find on the masthead) with a well-written and thorough one-page proposal letter: i.e., not 'I'd like to do a piece for you on plastic surgery for pets. Love Tessa'. But the issues, the 'story' (why it's interesting), the 'news angle' (why it's current), what makes you the person to write it (some link between you and the story).

Books are a fabulous resource and should be everyone's first stop. I directed her to check out some of the how-to books on journalism in her library. I suggested she approached magazines for some kind of full-time work as an editorial assistant. And I told her to try to find a local journalist willing to meet for coffee so she could pick his or her brain about how they got into the profession. When we ended our chat we were both thrilled – her, because I had given her some very *practical* advice, which made her realise that becoming a journalist was within her grasp and an utterly realistic goal, and me because I felt all big and powerful and as if I actually knew something. We had just spontaneously acted out Rule One of turning your dream into a reality: find someone who has done it and ask them how. Because, at this stage, you don't *know* how. But somebody out there does, and you're probably less than six degrees separated from them. They might even be as randomly close as I was.

Some sort of guide is almost a mandatory requirement at the nascent stage of your career – for advice as well as inspiration. When I first started going to my local open mic at an Upper West Side jazz bar, Cleopatra's Needle, the woman who ran it, a singer called Trudi Mann, called me at home and left a message saying how impressed she was with my singing. Her generous encouragement inspired me to keep coming. When I was there she frequently gave me helpful feedback and repertoire advice. And because I admired her singing, I took note. Even though sitting in the crowd awaiting my turn with the other singers was absolutely terrifying, I felt her support. It was a fabulous – and non-intimidating – introduction to singing in public.

HOT TIP
Enlist the help of a cheerleader. A friend who understands where you want to go and wants you to get there is invaluable. But it is also very important that they understand the difficulty of your endeavour and don't dent your enthusiasm (since this may be all that is keeping you going for a long time) by expecting too much, too soon. One of my friends inadvertently kept crushing my confidence at every piece of good news by not thinking it was enough. 'Vermont, ShVermont!' they said dismissively of what was a huge turnout and a musically successful night at an arts centre in Vermont. What they meant was: 'You deserve so much more!' But what it came across as was: 'You're not good enough!'

Moral support is everything at this stage. When I realised I was serious about making the change from writer to singer, I enlisted the help of a life coach, Mark Forster. Every week we'd speak on the telephone for half an hour and he'd give me feedback, techniques and tips on how to proceed. In my case – and maybe in yours – I had a lot of emotional blocks and fears to overcome which almost prevented me from being able to even see where I wanted to go. Mark helped me to overcome them with a brilliant but simple technique, which I use to this day.

Every day, at least once, I would write a page, or less, visualising a short-term goal exactly as I wanted it to turn out – for example, having a gig at a particular club, packed to the gills with a cheering audience, at which I am performing my absolute best. This was called the 'vision'. Then I would write a paragraph entitled 'present reality' giving a totally honest appraisal of where I was now. The vision had to be extremely detailed, describing my outfit, the crowd, their response, the lighting, how I looked, how I interacted with the band, how my voice sounded and – most important of all – how I *felt*. At first, I couldn't quite visualise what I wanted in my vision and my present reality was *always* gloomy: 'I feel like I'm crap . . . I'm scared no-one will come . . . I don't know what to wear . . . I don't know what songs to sing . . . I haven't even booked my musicians yet . . .'

As for results: in the beginning the actual event might not have measured up to my vision at all. But I would use the mistakes ('Drat! I forgot to mention the sound system in my vision!' or 'Hell! Forgot to write down how I wanted the lighting – *not* hospital bright!') to hone my next vision. Quite quickly the actual events started more and more closely to resemble my visions – no matter how 'unrealistic' the vision had seemed to me when I was writing it down. It was almost magical in its effectiveness. There were times when people would come up to me at the end of the evening and say *exactly*, word for word, what I had envisioned people saying.

Maybe there is such a thing as magic, or maybe writing out a clear vision of what I wanted made me prepare better. But it worked. It also stopped me micro-managing everything, by helping me keep the faith that things would just work out. That alone is more likely to *make* them work out. Think of the early days of growing a tomato plant. You've planted the seed and now you have to have faith (i.e., the belief in something you can't see yet) that it will grow into a bushy green plant with big red tomatoes hanging off it. You can't go watering it every ten minutes, or digging it up to see if it's got shoots yet, however strong the temptation.

I used to interfere like this all the time in my early days as a writer. Unless I had written a good first paragraph (i.e., could see the shoots of the future plant straight away), I simply couldn't progress to the next paragraph. This was all fine and dandy when I miraculously wrote a great opening. However, if I didn't, I could get snagged on the rusty nail of a bad first paragraph for weeks, as the deadline loomed terrifyingly nearer and nearer. It wasn't until a friend taught me that the best way to sit down and write anything was to allow yourself (almost expect yourself) to write crap, with the proviso that you can revise it later on, that I learned to let the seed actually grow a leaf or two before I started pruning away at it.

THE MEDUSA STARE

Don't listen to friends when the Friend inside you
says, 'Do this.'
Gandhi

One of the hardest things to get over when you switch careers is what I call 'the Medusa stare' – that look from your friends and family which turns you to stone and fixes you where you are. It's the pernicious idea that you couldn't possibly be good at one creative thing, let alone more than one. A few years ago I was unceremoniously fired by the editor who took over from the one who'd hired me a few months before to be the New York correspondent for a soon-to-be-launched in-flight magazine, even though he had never read a word of my writing. 'I hear you're a singer, and a good one at that,' he said. 'What kind of *writer* can you possibly be?' I didn't even get to send him samples of my work.

And when I first started out as a singer, people who hadn't heard me yet said exactly the same thing about my singing. 'How can you be a journalist *and* a singer?' Well, how about by actually *doing* both? If you do one thing well, the assumption is always going to be that anything else you do is going to be second rate. We've all heard the expression: 'Jack of all trades, master of none.' But that's no reason to believe it. The fact is, there are many people out there who are good at more than one thing, so don't limit yourself, or let other people limit you, by buying into it. Actor Gary Oldman's brilliant *Nil By Mouth*, which he both wrote and directed, is probably one of the best films he's ever made – never mind that he wasn't actually acting in it.

When Renee Knight, the former director of serious documentaries for programmes like *The Late Show* on the BBC, showed her first screenplay to a friend, her friend was absolutely blown away by how good it was. This surprise at your hidden talent is to be expected of friends, perhaps even more than the rest of the world. I think my friends felt a similar surprise when they first heard me sing. Don't take it personally. It's perfectly normal for people to feel like this. This is merely the first tier of the doubts you will encounter as you follow your path. Use the experience to help prepare you for later stings. But don't let it put you off. Enjoy surprising them.

When I confided in a cousin (who now loves my singing) that I wanted to be a singer he totally dismissed it as nonsense and told me a terrible story about his ex father-in-law having similarly 'set straight' some poor neighbour who asked his advice about whether he should try to be an opera singer. Of course not everyone who wants to is going to be able to sing or paint or write or whatever. But my cousin hadn't even heard me sing when he told me to give up. And even if he had, he wasn't the scriptwriter of my life, I was.

Or maybe I just used him as an excuse.

HOT TIP
Don't be one of those people who need permission from the rest of the world to be a happy, successful human being. You don't. You only need *your* permission. As my friend Mansur likes to say, 'Nobody can get in your way, except yourself!'

UNLOCK THE BLOCK

The winds of grace are always blowing,
but it is you that must raise your sails.
Rabindranath Tagore

As I now know, at each step you take you will feel anxious, depressed and tempted to remain with 'the devil you know' rather than strike out for the deep blue sea. I know a respected non-fiction writer who, about 10,000 words into two novels, has come to a standstill. After much pleading I was allowed to read the first. It is beautifully written, with brilliant characters, the dialogue is amazing, the story is hysterically funny and it made me laugh so hard that I had tears pouring down my face. That I read it for hours on my computer in my uncomfortable kitchen at two o'clock in the morning is a further testament to its brilliance. Then I was allowed to read the fragment of her second – a non-comic novel – which was even better. But she hasn't pursued a publisher. 'I care about it so much, I couldn't bear it if it got turned down,' she told me, when I asked what the hell she was playing at not taking it to her agent at once.

What she may know, either consciously or unconsciously, is that pursuing something that really means a lot to you; something that comes first in your life; something that is almost as precious to you as a child; something that essentially means putting your soul out there for anyone to stab at if they want to; something that means getting emotionally naked – well, it hurts. It brings out monsters in you that you never knew existed. Jealousy. Frustration. Shame. Fear. Obsessiveness. I met someone at a party recently who told me that she had become a journalist by default because writing a novel in her twenties had taken over her entire life. 'I couldn't think about anything *else*!' she said. 'I wouldn't want to be like that again.'

Rachel started writing plays when she was forty, having given up being a music producer when she moved to 'the middle of nowhere'. She also couldn't finish anything at first. She had lots of notes and story lines and characters but no finished plays. Now that she has completed two I asked her what stopped her before. 'Fear of failure. Fear of failure. Fear of failure,' she says. 'If you never complete anything you can never really fail. In the end it was just a matter of not giving up and keeping on doing it.' Her next task is to send them to a few theatre directors.

Writing plays is one thing. Having them produced is something else entirely. When I was a fledgling journalist I got so comfortable writing pitch letters, honing them to perfection, making them almost an end in themselves, and getting rejection letters in return, that when I had my first big commission I was terrified. I did all the research but it took me three weeks to begin the writing, which gave me a week to write the actual piece. But I was ready. I had paid my dues, I felt, and I'd had mini-successes along the way, so it felt *deserved*.

However, when, only two years into my new career as a singer (at the time, performing about five times a year in a noisy jazz bar on the Upper West Side), a major label expressed interest in me, I was most decidedly not ready. I got the initial message expressing their interest on my voicemail and was convinced it was a friend playing a prank, until I got home and saw it on my caller ID. Then I had a phone call from the Vice

President of A&R in which he told me that my voice was 'the most profoundly moving' he had heard *in the past ten years*. 'I'm sure you know what it means to say that,' he added. 'Means? Yes! It means . . . well, I'm not *sure* what it means, but whatever it is, I'm sure it's *bad*,' I thought. I was flung into a complete panic. One day on the subway, feeling perfectly happy with life, I suddenly remembered his phone call and literally sank down in the seat with my head in my hands, a feeling of utter dread welling up in my stomach. 'Don't come! I'm not ready,' I said the next time we spoke, all in a tizz. He just laughed.

When they came out to see me (three times, I think – although I was never entirely sure because I had no idea what he looked like) I was unprepared and nervous as hell. This was before I was being coached by Mark Forster and I didn't have my magic vision-writing technique to help calm me down. For some reason (quite possibly related to the aforementioned utter dread feeling) I had chosen to wear a pair of killingly tight shoes, and (ever wary of those people who don't know better being eager to dismiss me as 'just a dress') to totally change my style from sophisticated strapless-gowned *woman*, to please-take-me-seriously-as-a-jazz-musician East Village *girl*!

I also chose to do brand-new songs, which meant reading the lyrics and for some reason (again!) I had the sheets on the floor, where I couldn't see them, instead of on a music stand. It was my very first gig in that particular club, with a real listening crowd – as opposed to the noisy drunken rabble at the jazz club/sports bar I was used to. I was so nervous that at one point I spoke into the mic stand, forgetting that I had the actual mic in my hand. Perhaps not surprisingly, the A&R man reported back to me that I was 'curiously slightly less moving in person' than I had been on the demo. And here is where I made fatal error Number Two. I told him that he valued something (the demo) that I'd knocked out in four hours for $250 with no rehearsal and with a pianist I didn't even know. That if I could do that for $250, imagine what I could do with the thousands that labels usually spend on making a CD. And that *everyone else* preferred me live.

This is called 'Telling Someone How to Do Their Job', which is probably never a good idea. 'When in doubt, lay out!' as jazz singer Sheila Jordan tells her students about improvising over the music. The *correct* thing to say would have been something along the lines of what Keira Knightley said to director John Maybury, who turned her down for a movie saying: 'I know there's been a lot of hype about you but I don't think you can act and I don't want you in my movie.' She said: 'You say I can't act, and I'm not one hundred per cent sure I can either, but I'd love a shot at this part.' She got it.

HOT TIP
Be prepared to feel anxious and afraid as you get ready to move to the next level. Just don't let it stop you. So-called 'fear of success' is really just fear of change, or fear of failure. The fear won't disappear but you can manage it.

EASY DOES IT

If the creator had a purpose in equipping us with a neck,
he surely meant us to stick it out.
Arthur Koestler

There's a lot to be said for easing yourself into your new career. Of course you have to break out of your comfort zone, as Susan Jeffers points out in *Feel the Fear And Do It Anyway*, but there are times to move ahead in small increments and times to plunge in.

I sometimes get nervous before performances but it doesn't stop me any more. I have enough successful gigs behind me now to help me realise that I'll probably be 'all right on the night'.

Jodi Smith was earning upwards of $100,000 a year as a camera assistant when she decided to take a chance on being a screenwriter. For the past couple of years she has lived on savings and a part-time job, doing secretarial work for the painter Bridget Riley two days a week, in order to spend four hours a day on her writing. Jodi is in it for the long haul. 'My dad's a writer so I think I have a realistic idea of what is involved. The majority of people slog their guts out and bleed through their forehead before they make it. It's important to remind yourself of that. People like Quentin Tarantino, who wrote *Reservoir Dogs* in six weeks, are the exception.'

'You just have to keep your focus,' says Simon Robinson, whose business of designing and making papier mâché mirrors using a seventeenth-century technique is in its infancy. 'It takes a lot of mental discipline to not panic.' Best-selling author Alex Kershaw started out as a journalist at twenty-one and it took four or five years for that career to become self-supporting, working round the clock. 'Even then I was just getting by,' he says. 'But I had a chance and I wanted to take it. In the end it comes down to the question of what do you want to do for the rest of your life. If you compromise you'll always regret it.'

Keith Jarrett sums it up: 'I believe a truly valuable artist must be an artist who realises the impossibility of his task – and then continues to do it.'

How you can do it, too

1. Find someone who is doing it already and ask their advice. And don't feel bad about it. You will be doing them a favour, by reminding them of how far they've actually

come. Not everyone wants to share their experience, however. If the person you ask doesn't want to help you don't give up, find someone else. There is somebody out there for you.

2.   Identify each step in a short-term career plan within a certain time frame. Once I got to a certain level – regular (but low-paying) gigs, a growing fan base, a good reputation among musicians – I knew where I *was* and I had a picture of where I wanted to *be* (the success level of say, Cassandra Wilson or Diana Krall). But not being able to identify the steps in between kept me stuck where I was.

3.   To help you identify the next level, use a trick that Mark Forster taught me. Imagine a dialogue between the person you want to be and the person you are – in which the person you *are* interviews the person you want to be about how they got there. You'll be surprised at what you will turn up.

4.   Do ask other people who are a few levels ahead of you in your field what they think your next step is. Most people will be generous enough to tell you. People with whom you are running neck and neck may not feel so eager to help. I had a teacher once who seemed to be furiously jealous of all her students' successes. It was understandable. She was very talented and had somehow missed the boat, after having some good luck early in her career, when she was taken on by a major label who didn't know what to do with her.

5.   Be prepared to lose 'friends' along the way. Don't be afraid that people won't like you any more. This fear can really hold you back. But, believe me, anyone who does not want to see you happy is not your friend. When I first sent out a happy email after a particularly successful evening, thanking everyone on my mailing list for supporting me I

was absolutely crushed when one woman wrote and asked to be removed from the list. But, with a friend's help, I realised that this person should not have been on my list in the first place.

6. Expect to lose momentum from time to time. But notice when it happens and get back on track as soon as you can. Perhaps you need to take a break. That's fine. Just don't make it too long – i.e., anything more than a month. The life of an artist is so hard that many people completely 'check out'. I have seen so many jazz musicians fall by the wayside through drug abuse or simply giving up. Anything to stop feeling the pain. So-called 'making it' is a lifetime's work. Success in the creative arts requires consistent, long-term effort. Persistence.

7. Keep a record of each step you take towards your goal. When I first started sending pitch letters to editors, I made a table to keep a record of what the idea was, when I sent it, to whom and what, if any, was their response. Looking back over this list gave me a sense of how hard I was trying, as well as helping me keep track of who I had approached, so I knew how to follow up.

8. Be realistic. Don't imagine that you are going to make it 'overnight'. Unrealistically high expectations probably account for more people giving up than low expectations. Most artistic careers involve a great deal of work. You have to practise your art and since, especially in the early days (no matter how old you are), you are constantly improving and finding your own 'voice', you probably don't even *want* overnight success – unless you're only in it for the fame and glory. In jazz, the tortuous time you go through while you are honing your craft and living on subsistence level is called 'paying your dues'. If you don't pay them, you can't be a real jazz musician. It's the same in

any profession. Martin Amis's *The Rachel Papers*, written when he was in his early twenties, was a great first novel, but it is generally agreed that it wasn't until several novels later that he came into his own.

> Great dancers are not great because of their technique,
> they are great because of their passion.
>
> *Martha Graham*

Chapter Three:
I Will Survive: Supporting Yourself

I have no doubt that you're going to make it, Tessa. No doubt at all.
I'm just concerned that you'll die of starvation first!
My brother Simon, 2003

This chapter is about money – specifically how to sustain yourself while you pursue your creative dream. Nowadays anyone who claims to be an artist isn't really taken seriously unless they are making a living from it, even though it may actually be years before they 'make it' financially. Imagine meeting Van Gogh at a party today. 'An *artist*? Really? Are you *selling*? Do you have a gallery? Oh, you're planning to share a studio with an accountant-turned-painter named Paul? Uh, your *brother* has bought some of your work, you say?' When I first became a journalist in San Francisco, I'd rather sheepishly tell people who asked what I did that I was a journalist – feeling like a big liar because I actually earned my living from cleaning houses, and my 'journalism' was basically a volunteer job (i.e., unpaid work) eliciting rejection letters.

Of course, once I became a paid journalist I realised (from the standpoint of my 'before and after' perspective) that the fact I hadn't earned money from it before hadn't made me any less a writer. After all, how many poets make a living from writing poetry? The important thing was that I was writing at all. And, even more important, I was earning enough money elsewhere to sustain myself while I did it. But, of course, the ultimate goal was to be able to earn enough money doing what I loved (writing) for it to sustain itself.

There is no doubt in my mind that a period of time spent as a 'starving artist' focusing entirely on your dream is a good way to prove to yourself your commitment to your chosen path. In jazz they call this 'paying your dues'. But it isn't mandatory. In fact, living at subsistence level can be injurious to your success; leaving you financially unprepared to grasp opportunities when they appear (more on this later), as well as subjecting you to an unmanageable level of stress, which is detrimental to your health and performance.

'Not having enough money can drive anyone mad, sap energy, and channel creativity into imagining yourself living underneath a dank bridge somewhere with all your worldly goods stuffed into two carrier bags,' says Jane Lyle. 'Sometimes you have to earn money in other ways — and fit your art into the time you have left. I like to think of someone like Jane Austen, writing away in a corner, surrounded by her relations.' Reading biographies of artists, writers, dancers, musicians and actors reveals numerous examples of individuals who earned their living in other ways. It is vital to remember this and to separate who you are from how you make money when you need to. Then all you have to do is fit the dream into your schedule. 'See this as a creative challenge, rather than an onerous burden,' says Jane.

So banish all thoughts of romantically starving in a garret somewhere. Garrets are not romantic. Nor is starving. What *is* mandatory is that you spend time and energy on your chosen art, which means finding some way to support yourself while you do. The trick is to fund your creative dream with work that leaves you enough time and energy to devote to your chosen path, while at the same time support your basic financial needs. For me, cleaning houses while I strove to be a journalist was ideal. The hours were flexible. It was a means of regular income (very important for budgeting). And it wasn't either too emotionally and physically draining (leaving me no energy to write), or so comfortable that I was tempted to let up on my dream to make my living as a writer.

In fact, in that sense, it was even inspiring. David Mamet once said: 'If you have something to fall back on, you will.' Not me! Week after week plucking retch-inducing gobs of hair out of 'The Human Hairball's' drain (I had nicknames for all my clients), emptying 'The Puppy's' used condoms out of the trash in his bedroom, or down on my hands and knees cleaning 'The Bad German's' all-white (why, Inke, why white?), seventeen-foot-square kitchen floor with a dishwashing sponge (or *washing her light bulbs* – I think she deliberately dreamed up absurd cleaning jobs for me), was never going to be something to fall back on. Whenever I felt like giving up on being a writer, I only had to think about cleaning houses for the rest of my life to spring, gymnast-like, from floor to desk and write a proposal letter.

Ironically, when I was working as a magazine copy editor, in a previous incarnation, it was much harder to make time for writing. I'd often work twelve-hour days and weekends, working to tight deadlines, fitting copy to constantly changing layouts, rewriting bad copy, living in fear of finding typos after final proof stage (or – God forbid! – in the printed magazine once it appeared on the newsstands). I was on the go from the second I arrived at work until I walked out of the door at the end of the day. In the evenings I'd be too exhausted to do anything except cook for my family and flop passively in front of the telly. There was no question of sitting down to compose a proposal letter either at work or once I got home – which is probably why copy editors are paid well. I didn't start pitching story ideas until I became a freelancer.

But cleaning, although it wasn't lucrative, was work I could leave at work. I could choose my hours. And although I was broke and, at times, the grind was soul-destroying, my rent was cheap, my expenses were minimal (I dated for food) and I lived within my means. I didn't live *well*, exactly, but I wasn't in debt. This, I have since learned the hard way, is very important. Thank goodness I didn't have a credit card back then. Doing something creative for a living is already quite stressful enough without adding money worries to the list. And when you're broke (as you undoubtedly will be when you begin devoting your time to your dream), credit cards are nothing more than a nine-car pile-up waiting to happen. As I found out.

MAKE A STASH

It's a sad fact about our culture that a poet can earn much more money writing or talking about his art than he can by practising it.
W. H. Auden

In an ideal world, *you*, dear reader, will sensibly accrue savings before you make the transition to your new line of work. 'Build a financial reserve!' life coach Laura Berman Fortgang had admonished me time and again when I was still a struggling journalist. 'I know you won't like this, Tessa, but it's time to get a part-time job to keep yourself afloat.' I didn't listen. When I made the transition from writer to singer, my yearly income dropped about $10,000 as a musician-journalist, which didn't even cover my rent, let alone my expenses. And the following year, my worst, I made an $11,000 loss. When you are this broke, with neither savings nor a not-too-demanding source of regular income, the temptation to use credit cards as a 'stash' can be overwhelming.

Being a musician has shown me sides of myself that I didn't

even realise existed – both good and bad. But more than anything I've ever done, it has taught me (by depriving me of it) the value of money. Bit by painful, torturous bit. 'You've got who as your manager? Are you kidding me? You'll be signed to a major label any day now. Don't worry about money. Get one of those zero per cent credit cards and focus on your music,' said my singer friends, when they heard I'd been signed to a reputable manager. Naturally, I listened to these friends rather than that *other* kind: those gloomy, raggedy-clothed ones jumping up and down in the background waving and shouting: 'No! Stop! Don't do it!' Because I *knew* that of course, now that I had professional assistance, I'd be able to pay it all back, and soon.

This is called 'counting your chickens before they are hatched'. In fact, having a manager didn't really do anything for me at all, except make me feel good about myself for a while. Suffice to say here, the truth is that big-time managers and agents, especially those with large client lists, are often too busy with the artists that are already earning money for them to devote much attention to those who are in the development stage of their career. This is entirely understandable. Most managers and agents are in it for the money. And why shouldn't they be? However, most artists are not in it for the money. Most artists are in it because they can't *not* be in it, which sets up an immediate power imbalance in favour of the agent or manager – never mind that they are supposed to be working on your behalf (albeit on commission).

Always remember that no matter how powerful a manager or agent is, it doesn't matter how much they talk the talk if they don't also walk the walk. When they take you on they owe it to you to do the work of a manager/agent on your behalf, and if they don't deliver what they've said they will within a certain period, move on. Whatever you do, don't do what I did and wake up one morning to realise that a whole year has managed to slip by without you (and probably them too) realising. And during that year, although I was frantically busy – busier than I'd ever been as a writer (even when I was cleaning houses at the same time), and flagrantly investing in my music, I just wasn't earning enough money to live. So I simply *had* to live on credit. Or so I told myself.

With hindsight, I now see my credit card spending as akin to gambling with money borrowed from the mob. By the time I'd used up five zero per cent credit cards (two years later, that would be twenty-seven per cent, by the way, plus late and overlimit fees of $70 per card per month), I was in the worst financial trouble of my life – in credit card hock to maxed-out level and (with interest) mounting, plus what I owed to friends and family. Supplementing my income with my credit cards did allow me to focus on my music, in a way that simply would not have been possible had I been working on journalism full time – a round-the-clock endeavour if you're to make any kind of a living. But at great, *great* cost to my peace of mind.

HOT TIP

Don't use credit cards or loans to fund your career without having a clear idea of exactly how and when you will be able to pay it back. If friends loan you money, write out a short contract of the terms, stating when and at what interest rate (if any) you will repay it.

'Credit card companies have become the modern equivalent of the artistic patron,' says my actor friend Angus, who accumulated debts in excess of £70,000 during an eighteen-month stint while he focused solely on his acting career. Ultimately, for Angus, it worked out. First he went to a credit consolidation company, which got his payments down to £600 a month. And then he got a lucky break. 'I suddenly got £60,000 for an advertisement,' he says. 'It was literally like someone taking a burden off my shoulders.' But Angus was lucky. And he knows it. Because the truth is, credit card companies are not artistic patrons. And, *unlike* real artistic patrons (I've had a few of those too), they want paying back with interest.

Fast forward five years from getting my first article into British *Vogue* to the Pizza Express, Dean Street in London, one of the UK's most prestigious jazz venues. I'd just finished my last of a two-night run, singing to a totally packed house, which had been sold out a week in advance. My picture was on the enormous poster in the window. I'd been Pick of the Week in the jazz section of the *Guardian* Weekend Guide two weeks in a row. And I'd had a star review in *Time Out*. Terry Jones, of *Monty Python*, had come with his wife and two friends – including Geoffrey Burgon, who wrote the music for *Life of Brian*. 'No pressure!' I'd joked when we were introduced. And a dozen or so strangers had enthusiastically clustered around me at the end of the night to have me autograph my CD for them.

A week later, arriving back home in New York, I floated past my doorman. 'How was your trip?' he said. 'Wonderful! Wonderful!' I trilled, as I got into the elevator. Upstairs, I pushed open my front door, imagining the celebratory feast of chocolate Hob-nobs and PG Tips that awaited me as soon as I could unpack. And there on the mat was a note. Well, not a note exactly. Okay, not a note at all. Actually, more of an eviction notice for being three months late with the rent (again!). During this period I also had my electricity cut off for non-payment, and my phone, and I was enduring up to ten phone calls a day from the various credit card companies to whom I owed money. I slumped on to the arm of my couch, crumpling into tears. Here I was, an evening-gowned, autograph-signing, *Time Out*- and *Guardian*-recommended, poster-in-the-window, flat broke, financial disaster.

I think at that point I might have given up if I hadn't felt I now owed it to all the people who believed in me to keep going. Friends along the way have printed my demo for me, loaned me money, taught me Adobe Photoshop, given me a PC and a laptop, helped me design and maintain my website, all for free. Let alone devoted endless hours to supporting me emotionally. My first manager (also a talented producer) donated three hours to helping me do the final mix on my CD. My second manager loaned me the money to get it out of hock. I won a scholarship to the Manhattan School of Music – although I left after I met legendary jazz vocalist Mark Murphy who, for four years, taught me for free in return for running his workshops. *And* I'd also had six months of free lessons from the great jazz singer Sheila Jordan.

I couldn't give up now. Besides which, once it takes a hold of you, the 'curse' of music for musicians is that we do it because we're driven. We're like the girl in the Hans Christian Andersen story 'The Red Shoes' who can't stop dancing once she puts on the magical red ballet shoes. And I'm sure this feeling applies to whatever your passion is – acting, dancing, music, writing, painting, sculpting. As Miles Davis, in his autobiography, *Miles*, wrote: 'Music has always been like a curse because I have always felt driven to play it. It has always been the first thing in my life and it still is. It comes before everything.' I had read this quote long before I became a musician. Had I actually *understood* it, I'm not sure I would have started. It now resonates so strongly with me, I made a painting of it, which hangs in my sitting room.

Music is almost like an addiction. The more I do it, the more I need to do it. Music is my passion. It's like having a new baby: it requires (and slavishly gets) all my attention. And, like a baby, there's no question of 'fitting it in to my routine'. I have to fit in with *it*. And the tantalising carrot of 'when I get my deal' had fooled me into thinking I could rack up my credit cards and pay it all back by the time the interest rate kicked in. But I should have had a *plan*.

So what could I have done instead? Well, with hindsight I now see that attempting to do freelance features journalism at the same time as be a singer was doomed from the start, because both require a huge amount of effort to get work. Before I really started focusing on music I should have devoted six months or a year to establishing myself as a home interiors journalist – easy, fun and well paid. Or I could have got a part-time job that paid regularly but which was flexible and undemanding and covered my bills and rent. Waitressing, for example. The main thing was to have got this in place *before* I started on the stressful business of 'making it' as a jazz singer. Then, by the time I'd got so busy with my music that I couldn't think straight, the extra work would have been chugging along, sustaining itself (and me!) without too much effort.

As Veronica Henry says, 'Don't give up your day job!' Many signed authors find themselves with a deal, and an advance, but no idea of whether they are ultimately going to sell and become a success, and therefore go on to sign another deal. 'It's a delicate balance to keep. Throwing yourself into your writing, but at the same time not burning your bridges,' she says. Inevitably, in an attempt not to burn bridges one has to burn the midnight oil instead. 'But keep all the balls in the air until such a time as the sales figures say "Okay. Relax. Change the occupation slot on your passport to Author. It's official!" It took me two years to get the confidence to convince myself that I was a successful novelist, and have the nerve to turn down TV commissions,' says Veronica. 'Also, having another hat on can often be a source of material. And even a release.'

Cairo-based novelist Alaa El Aswany, whose *The Yacoubian Building* is one of the most successful Middle Eastern books of all time (it is currently being made into a movie), would not dream of giving up his day job as a dentist. 'I don't expect to make enough money to live on as a writer. But also I like my profession,' he says. 'I work here in the day on patients and I write at night in the same office. I feel they are the same world. I am always dealing with people, with characters in both professions.'

JUST *DON'T* DO IT!

The trouble with being poor is that it takes up all your time.
Willem de Kooning

As it was, I bought groceries and paid bills with my credit cards until I maxed them out and couldn't pay the minimums any more, which was not only stressful, even irresponsible, it was injurious to my success. As Steven Covey writes, in *The Seven Habits of Highly Effective People*: 'Economic security is basic to one's opportunity to do much in any other dimension.' When that major recording label showed interest in my music, barely two years into my career, over a demo CD recording that I had made in a morning for a mere $250, I was entirely unprepared. I had just taken a full-time job in an attempt to catch up on my overwhelming pile of debts and bills, and I simply did not have the required energy or ability to think straight to make the most of that opportunity.

I actually did get used to it, but it was hard for the first few months. 'How do people do this thing called full-time work?' I asked friends. '*And* do the laundry, clean their homes and have lives?' Getting up at 7 a.m. (having fretted the night away stressing about having to get up at 7 a.m.) was killing me. Sitting in front of a computer all day transforming long inaccurate descriptions of New York City restaurants, clubs and shops into short inaccurate descriptions, then getting home at 7 p.m. and writing freelance articles for magazines in the evenings (all things I would happily have done for my writing career before) was sucking the life out of me. And commuting! Travelling at peak hours, my face crushed up against the glass of the door between subway carriages, then having to karate chop my way through the crowd to get out at my stop before they closed the doors on me (sometimes literally) . . . Hey, I'm a musician. We don't do rush hour! And we *never* get up at 7 a.m!

On top of that, unaccustomed to office germs, I was in a constant state of either recovering from, or fighting off, a cold or flu. Not good for a singer. Your body is your instrument. Let's just say that the three times the label came to see me perform live I was not at my best. It's not their job to make allowances for you being ill and/or exhausted. If they've never seen you before, they can only judge you on what you present them with on the night. But had I been able to take time off work to focus on the gigs: to rehearse the band, to hire a consultant to help me negotiate the label's interest and advise me on what to wear, what to perform, who to perform with, it might have made all the difference. But I couldn't. I was desperately trying to catch up on back rent, overdue bills and minimum credit card payments, I couldn't take time off work without losing pay, and I didn't have a red cent to spare for anything else.

The fact is, using credit is all well and good if you have a regular income and can strategise paying it back. I used to know a woman who lived in constant debt (usually quite substantial) to the tune of exactly what she was owed in freelance earnings – never more or less. It was stressful, but manageable. In fact, that was how, in a small way, I lived in San Francisco as a journalist. I occasionally borrowed the rent from a friend, knowing that I was due to get a payment from a magazine who had accepted one of my pieces (they usually take from one to three months to pay).

Once I got up and running as a writer, as long as I was ahead of the game, I could even branch out a little. I became a member of the Writers' Grotto, a writers' collective in San Francisco started by Ethan Watters, Ethan Canin and Po Bronson, renting a tiny office for $300 a month. Ethan Watters had predicted that I would earn more money, '. . . just because you have to pay the office rent.' And he was right. Renting the office turned out to be a good investment, because – away from the temptations of home – a fridge full of food, the telephone, cleaning for procrastination, I worked twice as hard. By 1997, when I moved to New York, I could earn three times my rent in a good month. But my singing career had come upon me so suddenly and unexpectedly that I was unprepared.

IF YOU WANT IT, GO AND GET IT

The fact that writers will go through so much to remain writers says something, perhaps everything. It would be far easier (and nearly always more profitable) to become a real estate agent.

Maria Lenhart

Michael Becker is good example of doing it right. He mortgaged his home to help fund his career change from producer, musician and composer (he co-wrote and produced the song that accompanies the credits to the movie *Crash*) to photographer. 'Last month was the first month I thought, "This month I want to make enough money to pay the rent."' There was no reason to think that would happen, he says, but then – through a lucky break – he got a job taking photographs for ABC Television plus a royalty payment for some music he had written for Disney seven years ago. 'And miraculously I had the mortgage money.'

Which brings me to the happier subject of actually *making*

money from your creative pursuit. When I first started pitching articles to magazines I was absolutely willing to write for nothing. Luckily, since I started out writing for major publications (who offer set rates), it never came to that, but I did negotiate with one or two editors to write 'on spec' i.e., with a definite commission in terms of what they wanted, but with no promise of a kill fee if it turned out badly. This made it a low-risk (and, therefore, more attractive) proposition for them to hire me.

But there would have been nothing wrong with writing for free for small publications, if it *had* come to that, in order to build up my cuttings file. I know countless people who got into their chosen careers by volunteering their services to start with. TV show host Daphne Brogden started out as an unpaid intern on various Los Angeles radio and TV stations – supporting herself at the same time by working in a Los Angeles department store. When she finally did start getting paid it was a paltry $8.35 an hour. 'But it was so exciting to work at my dream job and get paid for it,' she says.

Eventually Daphne got hired to produce the Dr Dean Edell show on San Francisco's KGO Radio ('I was kind of Roz to his Frasier.'), where she also wisely donated her free time in order to reap financial benefits later on. 'I saw a need for extra duties and I did them for free. I added music to make it appeal to a younger market. I added a quiz. I did a *Daphne's Corner* spot. And I realised I was good! So one day I said, "Listen, I do a lot for the show that goes way beyond screening and I want a thirty per cent raise plus benefits." They offered me fifteen per cent with benefits with a big deductible.' However, knowing she'd made herself indispensable, Daphne held out. 'So they gave me what I asked for, provided I did some extra duties – which actually I was happy to do.'

HOT TIP
Be willing to work for nothing or very little to get a foot in the door. But don't do it for too long.

It is important to know what you're worth, as well as the going rate for what you're offering. When Michael had his first photography show, he made a decision not to charge what he calls 'quasi-wannabe' prices. 'You are either a gallery-represented artist or you're not and there are pretty standard rates, depending on how big a name you are,' he says. So, working on the premise that 'people put value on your work based on what it costs', he charged at the lower end of the going rate, *but no lower*. 'If I sold pictures through that gallery for two hundred dollars, then I couldn't start charging another gallery six hundred dollars.'

It helped that Michael wasn't broke and was able to keep up the show of independence that creates the illusion of being worth more, unlike the writer Balzac, who, when he was starting out, was offered 3,000 francs by a bookseller for his first novel. When he found out that Balzac lived in a poor part of town he dropped his offer to 2,000. When he saw that he lived on the top floor in the proverbial garret, he went down to 1,500 francs. Upon entering the room he caught Balzac dipping a stale roll in a glass of water. He dropped the price to 300 francs.

Michael also researched the financial side of his new career. 'Whereas in my approach to music I just got lucky, with my photography I read up on the business of it. I thought, "Okay, if I want to make a go of it, I really have to make a go of it,"' he says. 'I have learned that if you want to make a living at what you are doing, you have to be proactive. You have to do marketing. Not to do that is naïve. I used to be terrible at it but now I'm like, "This is my work, this is what I do, and now it's time to get paid for it!"'

If you can't do this for yourself, it is a good idea to get someone else to do it for you. When I first got my booking agent, Reggie, I was terrified that he would price me out of jobs by asking too much. However, the first job he got me paid more for one night than I would generally be paid for two weeks' work in the New York clubs. There is no way I would have asked for that on my own. Carol Hall, who wrote the musical score and lyrics for *The Best Little Whorehouse in Texas*, had similarly low expectations of her income. 'Then one day I walked in to my agent's office and heard him on the phone yelling: "It's one hundred thousand dollars or nothing!" before slamming the phone down. "Wow!" I thought. "He must handle some important people." "Who was that for?" I asked. He said: "Oh, you."'

How you can do it, too.

1. Make a monthly and yearly business plan before you take the leap. Include all anticipated outgoing expenses (food, transport, clothes, equipment and repairs, promotional materials, mailing costs, hired help, rent, telephone, heating etc., so that you have a clear picture of your cash-flow situation.

2. Be prepared. Don't allow yourself to get into a position where you are distracted from your purpose by serious financial concerns regarding day-to-day living. Make sure you have the resources to give any unexpected opportunities your best shot. If this means keeping your day job for a year or more until you have enough savings to leave it, or taking a part-time job to sustain you until you are earning enough money from your dream to support yourself, then so be it.

3. Educate yourself about the business of your chosen

creative career. In other words, know as much about the money side of your work as you do about your craft. What is your value? What is the going rate for the job? Creative people need to talk to other artists in their discipline to establish some kind of standard. Do the maths so you don't price yourself out of a job but also ask for what you are worth. And always know who you are dealing with. Some people can afford to pay more than others.

4. Ask for what you are worth but prove that you're worth it first.

5. Two freelance careers (journalism and music) are probably not a good idea, and neither are two jobs that draw from the same creative well. However, avoid jobs that are soul-destroying, isolating or decrease self-esteem.

6. If you are using your credit cards to live on, as I was, that is a warning sign that you'd better take time out for a while and establish some kind of regular income.

7. If you get into financial trouble, consult an expert. If you are already in credit card hell, consult a credit card consolidation agency. Your credit card company should be able to recommend one. Or consider bankruptcy.

8. Don't have an attitude. Even after you get the raise, make sure you still treat your boss as the boss or you won't get the next kick up. When Daphne was a screener she always made sure her boss had a glass of water on his desk. After she was promoted, she made sure he still got it.

9. Consider investing money in one-off professional counsel. If I had hired a consultant to coach me through the first label's interest in me I could have avoided some (in retrospect) obvious mistakes. Believe in yourself enough to make that investment. If you are wrong you will have wasted a little money. If you are right, then you will be glad you did.

10. Don't cut corners. My first demo was a miracle, I now realise. My first, self-produced CD, recorded in a 'bargain' studio without any rehearsal, was one of the most depressing and stressful – and expensive! – experiences in my life, even though it eventually turned out well.

11. Do invest in expert assistance whenever any type of production is involved. My CD was mixed in three separate studios before I finally enlisted the help of my former manager. She did in three hours what I, on my own with three separate engineers, had not been able to do over the previous six months. She didn't charge me, but it would definitely have been worth it even if she had.

12. If possible, set aside money to invest in education. I was lucky in having two legendary jazz singers as teachers and mentors. But a good knowledge of music theory is invaluable, and having a teacher moved me along far more quickly than teaching myself.

13. Finally: 'Do only what you love to do. You may go hungry, but you will totally live.' Elisabeth Kübler-Ross, *The Wheel of Life*

It'd be nice to make lots of money but it's quite difficult,
because every time I make lots of money I make a bigger piece
that costs lots of money.
Damien Hirst

Chapter Four:
The Long and Winding Road:
Keeping The Faith

The hardest thing was not learning to write;
the hardest thing was to *never give up*.
Po Bronson, What Should I Do With My Life?

This chapter deals with that point in pursuing your dream where you think you can't carry on any more. It may be that you have achieved some success, but it feels like it's not enough. Or maybe you thought you'd 'make it' sooner. Perhaps, at the height of what seems to be 'success', you feel profoundly depressed and, in the words of the Peggy Lee song, are thinking: 'Is that all there is?' Perhaps you're several years in, wondering what the *hell* you were thinking when you started down this road. Maybe, after months or years of being stuck at the same level, you've reached a point where you feel like you are bashing your head against a brick wall and are ready to throw in the towel.

It's easy to keep going when things feel good. The challenge is to keep going when it *stops* feeling good. This chapter is about how to get unstuck, as well as how to keep going when you lose faith, when you feel as if you reached rock bottom a long time ago but keep finding – no! – there's still a ravine or two to go. As Katherine Mansfield wrote, 'When one thinks: "Now I have touched the bottom of the sea – now I can go no deeper" one goes deeper . . . the suffering is boundless.' Then the challenge is to remember what she wrote in a happier mood: 'There is no feeling to be compared to having written and finished a story.'

Because, wherever you are, be it near or far from your dreamed-of destination, the endeavour is so difficult, so fraught with doubts, so peppered with failures along the way, at times it feels like it would be easier to give up. To keep going requires constant effort, confidence, self-belief, preparation, a road map, assistance and encouragement from the people around you, a *plan*. Too many talented people give up, not because they don't have the talent, but because they don't have the discipline to keep going.

My friend Jay is an extraordinary writer. My friend Joe is an amazing singer. My friend Maria is a wonderful photographer with a natural eye for composition. They all love doing it. They all *started* doing it – not as a profession yet but with a view to making it a profession one day. But somewhere along the way they stopped. They have allowed themselves to be waylaid by self-doubt and fear. As Maria told me when I asked her what on earth she was thinking by giving up on photography before she'd really begun: 'I just don't have the guts, Tessa.' And I know how she feels. There are days (okay weeks, maybe months!) when I am so tired of being a musician I can't even *listen* to music, let alone make any.

Following a creative dream requires you to ride out the bad times as well as the good, and that takes more than just talent. In fact, as Julia Cameron points out in *The Artist's Way*, 'All too often it is audacity and not talent that moves an artist to centre stage.' And just as often, maybe *more* often, it is lack of audacity, not lack of talent, which makes others give up. This feeling hits most artists at some point or other. If they're advanced in their efforts, momentum may be able to carry them through it. But if this feeling hits too soon in the process, far too many genuine talents give up, literally before they really began. This isn't to say, don't dream big. By all means, *do*. But if you don't dream realistically in terms of timing, you are likely to be disappointed early on when things don't 'happen' straightaway, and lose faith in yourself.

In my own case, when I first started singing in public, it was with very little ambition. I didn't really expect anything particularly to come of it. I was still working hard as a journalist (though not focusing on it as much as before I was singing), and singing was something I did for pure love. However, about two years into it, I gradually started to think maybe I could make 'something' of it because so many people seemed convinced that I could. Strangers would come up and say: 'You're going to be famous!' Occasionally, someone would even say they had a small label they wanted to put me on, which used to be very thrilling – until I'd find out that they didn't have a label at all, they just wanted to look important at that moment. And when a bona fide label expressed interest in me at around this time, I really started to think I could do it for a living.

Ironically, it was when I started to have expectations of it that my confidence fell away. Of course I hadn't expected to be discovered singing in the shower, but the attention I got soon after stepping on to a stage fostered the illusion that something would 'happen' in that magical time-frame known as 'overnight'. However, the momentum I started out with wasn't enough to keep me going for as long as (it turned out) I needed it to. Imagine a toy car pushed up hill. It may go up part of the way, but pretty soon it runs out of push and slides back down again. The minute you stop doing it just for love and start focusing on an outcome you are assailed with doubts and fears and you wake up and think the demoralising thought: 'My God. This isn't going to happen is it!'

This stage in your career is all about endurance and faith, keeping on putting one foot in front of the other. It's like doing a triathlon, as my friend Ruth, who took part in a charity triathlon event, discovered. The lessons she learned could be applied to any artistic career: both are ultimately a test of endurance and focus. For the record, before she started Ruth was not a gym rat. 'I ripped a hole in the knee of my brand-new running tights with my nail the very first day I bought them. My bike was a blue, little number from which I'd removed the front basket – definitely not a Lance Armstrong affair – and the first time I wore my bike helmet, my coach rolled his eyeballs and told me I had it on back to front.' But every oak tree starts with an acorn, as the saying goes. And finding out (after six long months of training) that she was capable of completing a triathlon was a big lesson – and confidence booster.

'But the achievement was *not* swimming for 1.5 kilometres in dark, frigid and jellyfish-infested waters, followed by 40 kilometres on my bike, followed by 10 kilometres of running up and down hills,' she says. 'It was winning the games that the self-destructive part of my mind, "The Quitter", had played on me for all those long, cold and lonely hours, when all I could focus on were the naysayers who'd looked at me in disbelief when I said I was doing this thing – and I suspected they were right!' Ruth discovered that the way forward was just to keep going until, as she puts it, 'the rhythm takes over and supplants the voice of resistance, which is screaming full-decibel in your mind, "I can't ... I just CAN'T!" Ultimately, you find you *can*.' And therein lies the achievement.

It's about the journey, not the destination. What Ruth learned, was that she didn't need to 'win' to gain the benefits. 'Any triathlete will tell you that the way to succeed is to pay attention to your own race, and not let yourself be distracted by the performance of others: there are three long and difficult events, and while someone else could be a far better swimmer than you, they may not be a speed cyclist. They could be a great cyclist, but may have spent all their leg energy during that stage of the race and have nothing left for the punishing final run. The race is with yourself, and that means it's not even really a race – it's just about sticking to the plan and staying the course.'

Imagine asking someone who has just got in from doing a marathon, say, whether they 'won'. And yet, rather than do what we are supposed to do (i.e., be in the moment, focus on achieving a personal best), we do that to ourselves in our artistic endeavours all the time. And it's a killer.

HOT TIP
Take up some form of physical exercise. Not only will it focus your mind on something other than your work, it will teach you endurance. You don't have a run a marathon. Just commit to doing even five minutes on the exercise bike, running to the corner shop – even briskly walking just one block, as long as it's a challenge. Whatever you do, make it just beyond your reach and then prove to yourself that you *can* keep going.

HANG ON TO YOUR LOVE

Magic is believing in yourself, if you can do that,
you can make anything happen.
Goethe

'People talk about following your bliss,' says Simon Robinson, the mirror maker. 'But sometimes when you do that and you have to "play the game" – pandering to shop buyers who don't want to buy anything that hasn't already been in a magazine – you end up hating the thing you once loved. It becomes such brutal grinding work that you don't want to think about it any more.' I know what he means. I got to a stage in my music where I was so focused on turning it into something that would make me a living, I forgot why I was doing it in the first place – for love; for its own sake; because I just loved doing it in the moment.

'There should always be a sense of moving ahead and growing all the time,' says Michael Becker, the former musician and producer turned photographer. 'But you absolutely positively can't be focused on the end result.' Interestingly, since Michael started focusing on his photography and, consequently, relaxed about his music (which had been falling by the wayside for some time before he took up photography), his music career has been quietly taking off again – most notably with the song 'In the Deep', which he co-wrote and produced (and played all the instruments on) with singer-actor Bird York, playing out the end of the movie *Crash*.

But photography is now his first love, and he has faith in it turning out well – to the extent that he was willing to mortgage his house at the beginning. 'I'm not sure I knew where I was going, but I knew I was going somewhere,' he says. And having researched his career thoroughly, he was prepared for it to take a long time. 'It was something I read over and over again on the websites I looked at. It takes time.'

'When I got out of college I thought it was just a Hollywood cliché that you have to suspend your overnight success story,' says film maker David Munro, whose film *Full Grown Men*, starring Deborah Harry and Alan Cumming, was in production at the time we spoke. 'But ten years into it I realise that it's true, and that when you dig a little deeper you find that everyone who is successful has been doing it for years.' David is now in a place where he feels relaxed about the outcome. 'Once I let of the feeling of entitlement I became a lot happier o productive,' he says. 'Worrying all the time abou happening takes up a lot of energy. My stress was all about what it all meant and how it should translate into money and success.'

Once David saw what he was doing, he began to concentrate on specific tasks and what inspired him. 'When I realised I was chasing geese, saying, "Maybe this project, or this project?" I pulled back and thought about my approach and that's when things started to happen.' Even so, he says, 'I don't think I'll ever be able to get so Zen about it that I think just the journey is enough. It takes money to live and you do need that ego and that confidence to keep going forward.' The main thing is that he now realises that his initial game plan of 'two to three years *max*' out of college was somewhat unrealistic.

He learned about endurance from the experience of pursuing his wife, now also his producer, Xandra Castleton. 'It took about a year to win her over. And lots of people told me to give up on her but I didn't,' says David. 'If I *had*, I would always have felt, "What if I'd hung in there?" That would have been what Florence Scovel-Shinn, in her wonderful esoteric book, *The Game Of Life and How To Play It*, would liken to someone digging for treasure and giving up 'three feet from the gold'. At times it may feel more like you're chasing 'the carrot before the donkey', lusting after the unobtainable which remains tantalisingly only just out of reach. But there's a huge difference, if you can remind yourself of it; with your creative endeavour you get to enjoy it along the way. You just have to, as David says, 'adjust your clock a bit'.

And keep reminding yourself of why you are doing this. Interior designer Susan Cozzi says, 'It seems as if every day I lose the faith. I constantly have to repeat mantras of confidence and optimism: "You're excellent at what you do." "You're amazing with colour." "Just remember how pleased the client was with your work."' Alex Kershaw, author of two *New York Times* best sellers, who started in journalism at the age of twenty-one writing for free, got somewhere in the end. Alex has had two of his books and an idea for a book optioned in Hollywood. 'But it took eighteen years to get here. People need to know that it takes that long,' he says. 'So you have to really enjoy what you're doing. If you keep practising you'll get good at it and you'll eventually get somewhere.' The alternative – doing something he didn't enjoy just for money – doesn't bear thinking about.

JUST KEEP HOLDING ON

Never give in! Never give in! Never, never, never. Never – in anything great or small, large or petty – never give in except to convictions of honour and good sense.

Winston Churchill

I have many, many times wanted to give up being a musician. It's so emotionally exhausting at times. But then I'd think, 'What about all those people I'd be letting down?' The people who have loaned me money, been my cheerleaders, talked me down from the window ledges of despair countless times. The other thing that keeps me going is an inherent belief in what I am doing. Oh, and the need to express myself and be understood by the people I am expressing myself to.

Because when you get down to it, that's what creative expression is all about. It's like smiling. Of course there are times when you are overcome with joy at something when you're all alone somewhere, and it feels wonderful and you just can't help smiling. But if you smile *at* someone, it's important that they smile back. Sometimes I think it's like making love. More than half the pleasure you get from the experience is gained from the pleasure you are giving to the other person. Talking about his spiritual awakening, John Coltrane said: 'I humbly asked to be given the means and privilege to make others happy through music.'

Always remember that this is what you're there for, whether you are acting, painting, making films or furniture. After Martha Graham's first solo performance, a woman came backstage afterwards and said, 'Martha, this is simply dreadful. How long do you expect to keep it up?' Martha replied, 'As long as I have an audience.' After her performance of 'Lamentation' another woman came backstage to Graham afterwards and said, 'You will never know what you have done for me tonight. Thank you.' Her son had recently been killed and she had been unable to cry until she watched 'Lamentation'. 'What I learned that night is that there is always one person in the audience to whom you speak,' said Graham.

'You have to have a certain level of belief in the core values of what you are doing. It's what we do with our mirrors,' says Simon Robinson. 'They are made with love, and a lot of care. That belief in the core value of what you do is what makes you keep it up. It's what keeps you centred.' It's like cooking. Not many people like cooking for themselves, but cooking for other people is about love – whether you are a chef or just cooking for friends or family. Similarly, my songs and performances are delivered with love i.e., I love singing the songs, planning which ones to sing, putting them into a coherent order, thinking about the audience and what they might enjoy, what of *what I have to give* might cheer them up or be cathartic.

I did a gig abroad once that lasted twelve days. As soon as I got off the plane I went down with flu, which meant spending all day groaning in bed and getting up at night just to perform. The musicians the club provided were not up to par – particularly for someone who'd been so utterly spoiled by working with New York musicians. The crowd was noisy. The sound system, which would be perfect when I went in to fix it (myself, mind you!) in the daytime, was mysteriously terrible at night and made my voice (my instrument) sound about as good as a saxophone that had been left out in the rain all night, which threw me off completely – it was like trying to sing with someone else's voice.

And my style of music – clearly evident on the CD that had got me the gig in the first place – was 'wrong for the club', I was informed by the booker. He took me aside on the second night. 'Tessa, there is a problem,' he said. 'Your music is the kind of music people have to listen to. The owner wants you to do the blues.' If I hadn't believed in myself and my music this would have been an utter disaster – not least because I don't sing the blues. Thousands of miles from home with another ten days to go, I don't know how I'd have coped with it emotionally in the early days of my singing career. Probably imploded.

However, I handled it. I hired a totally new band – younger and more hip, who understood and appreciated the vibe I was trying to get. I worked out that the problem with the sound system was that it reset itself every time you switched it off, so I fixed it every afternoon and made sure nobody touched it until the end of the night. I also wrote down exactly the dial numbers so that if a disaster *did* happen I could reset it quickly. This reaction of just getting on with it is what's called 'being a professional'. In a basketball game, if someone on your team drops the ball, you don't stand around crying, saying, 'Hey, man. You dropped the ball!' There's no time. Your job is to get on with what needs to be done, grab that ball back and get it into the hands of someone who can make a basket as quickly as possible.

By the Friday night (four days later), the audience was loving it and cheering wildly – clearly not minding at all that it was *the sort of music you had to listen to*. When the owner and booker paid me at the end of the week they were thrilled, hugging me and congratulating me – and not mentioning (or perhaps even noticing) that I hadn't sung one blues song all week. It was also part of being professional, by the way, that I didn't helpfully point out to them how I'd proved them wrong. 'To know what you prefer instead of humbly saying Amen to what the world tells you you ought to prefer, is to have kept your soul alive,' wrote Robert Louis Stevenson. And, let's not beat around the bush here, when someone tells you how and what to write/paint/sing/act, it's your soul that's on the line. Once you've sold that you might as well give up.

> **HOT TIP**
> Join a support group, or form one yourself. There is even a Twelve-step programme for artists called Arts Anonymous. A spin-off from the original Alcoholics Anonymous Twelve-step programme, rather than get people to give up anything, they are encouraged to pick *up* their art. The title of one of the pamphlets, 'Facing Avoidance', says it all. Members enlist an 'art buddy' to hold them to promises to work on their art itself or on the business side of it.

When Alaa El Aswany had finished his novel *The Yacoubian Building*, it took a whole year to find a publisher in the Middle East because of the gay characters and the political issues. 'Every publisher said they loved it but that they would lose their job if they published it,' says Alaa. 'Finally I found what I call a "suicide publisher" in Beirut, and they put it out.' Since then it has been published in English. If he had given up after the first few publishers had turned it down, the world would have missed out.

'Giving up is just not an option,' says Simon Robinson. 'I am determined to make this work. Once you begin a project you don't give up on it. Never. There are many levels of pain you go through and sometimes you sink so low you don't think you could possibly go any further. But you do, and you survive. Once you get there your brain says: "Hey, it's not so bad. It's still manageable." As long as you remain sane and keep your sense of humour it's manageable. You have to keep your focus and just not panic.'

SATISFY YOUR SOUL

There is a vitality, a life force, an energy, a quickening, that is translated through you into action, and because there is only one of you in all time, this expression is unique.

Martha Graham

I learned all about panic from the original record label interest in me. Overnight I became a nervous wreck! From that first phone call and for the next six months, not knowing if they were going to be in the crowd or not, I stopped enjoying performances. I became concerned with what I was wearing, what songs I should do to impress them, what they might think of me. In other words, everything except what I *should* have been focused on – the moment, the music, the crowd, the sheer joy of what I was doing it. I was so concerned with what *image* I might be projecting that I totally forgot who *I* actually *was*.

The valuable lesson it taught me is that you can only be yourself. If people don't like you, fine. But second-guessing what someone may or may not like is death to creativity. As David Bowie said in a print ad for Audi, 'There is no progress without failure. And each failure is a lesson learned. Unnecessary failures are the ones where an artist tries to second-guess an audience's taste, and little comes out of that except a kind of inward humiliation.' I forgot that what the label had liked in the first place was my voice; my singing style, naked and unadorned: me. Not someone (else) I thought they perhaps wanted me to be.

What's for sure is that focusing on 'making it' will keep you from sticking to your path faster than anything. As Kenny Werner says in *Effortless Mastery*: 'Of all the people who pursue careers in music, be it jazz or classical, how many become stars? A musician's life is the riskiest investment in the universe. If it's money you're after, become a bank president.' This could be said of all the art forms – from music to interior design. Yes you have to make a living, but the main reason to be an artist is for its own sake. Michael the photographer says he'd be a waiter if that was what was required of him to be able to support his life as a photographer.

'If you are a struggling musician-artist, there are only three reasons you don't quit,' says Kenny Werner. 'One, you're having a lot of fun and you love the music THAT MUCH; two, you have a deep-seated need to express yourself through music; or three, you are either too lazy, too scared, or too dysfunctional to retrain for another career. I believe that if you are motivated by either of the first two reasons, or by both, you will be taken care of.'

HOT TIP
Keep going. It's normal to panic at the point of moving to the next level. Calm down and just keep putting one foot in front of the other. As my friend Sheila Cooper said to me when I decided that, just at the point that Ronnie Scott's finally booked me, I couldn't carry on any more: 'Don't stop! You're just confusing the brink of success with a precipice!'

Countless artists make it late in life. Mary Wesley published her first novel at seventy. Singer Sheila Jordan got signed to Blue Note Records at forty-five. Daniel Defoe published his first novel at fifty.

Pop diva Tina Turner made her comeback at around the same age. Comic actor Rodney Dangerfield made a spectacular comeback after taking a twelve-year break from show business during which time he sold aluminium siding. Impatience is the enemy of peace. 'It's as difficult to make a picture as it is to discover a diamond,' said Vincent Van Gogh. 'But whereas everyone knows the value of a golden louis or a fine pearl, unfortunately those people who know the value of pictures and believe in them are rare. Still such people do exist. Anyway, there's nothing better to do than sit and wait patiently, even if one has to wait a very long time.' Sadly, Van Gogh didn't live to see his success. Sadly for him, that is. Happily for *us*, he never allowed lack of success to make him give up, and his work lives on. Persistence is everything.

How you can do it, too

1. Banish all thoughts of 'overnight success'. If you dig a little deeper into any overnight success stories you hear, you will find that most of those people have been working on it for years. In fact, banish all thoughts of success, and focus on loving what you do for its own sake.
2. Imagine the alternative. Whenever she feels she can't carry on any more, jazz singer Kendra Shank says, 'I project myself into an alternative life and I see myself as very unhappy, and I realise that anything I pursue is going to have its own set of challenges.'
3. Take a break. Give yourself a week off working on your dream. Go to museums or for a walk in nature or to hear music. Singer-songwriter David Walmer says, 'Sometimes I might not have writer's block, but what I'm doing isn't new. That is a sign to me that I'm burnt out or trying too hard and that I *should* stop. That's when I look for inspiration outside of myself.'

4.   Go outside yourself for encouragement. I read somewhere that when Anthony Perkins felt down he would get dressed up and go walking in the street and get off on being recognised. I occasionally look at my CDBaby.com page where people write their comments. It doesn't matter how miserable and hopeless I feel, it always cheers me up.

5.   Take action, even when you don't feel in the mood. In *Jeff Galloway's Training Journal* for marathon runners, one of the inspirational quotes is: 'The most exhilarating runs are often on the stressed-out days when we don't want to run.' If I have practised a song even when I don't want to, I always feel better afterwards – probably even better than I'd have felt if I'd practised when I was actually in the mood. Treat yourself as a naughty child whose tantrum you are blithely ignoring while you go about doing the grocery shopping, in spite of the stares of other shoppers.

6.   Relax. Are you suffering from growing pains? About two years into my singing, I became profoundly depressed with where I was musically. I felt talentless and hopeless. In the middle of feeling like that I went to a workshop run by a singer called Ann Dyer. 'Oh that!' she said, comfortingly dismissive, when I confided in her how I was feeling. 'That just means you're getting ready to move to the next level.'

7.   Meditate. It will help you learn to focus on the all-important present moment, from which everything comes. 'Every moment is precious precisely because it is ephemeral and cannot be duplicated, retrieved or captured,' writes Stephen Nachmanovitch, in *Freeplay: Improvisation in Life and Art*.

We are made to persist. That's how we find out who we are.
Tobias Wolff

Chapter Five:
Love Me or Leave Me:
Negotiating Your Intimate Relationships

If a woman told us that she loved flowers,
and we saw that she forgot to water them,
we would not believe in her 'love' for the flowers.
Love is the active concern for the life and growth of that
which we love.
Erich Fromm, The Art of Loving

When I first started thinking about this chapter, I realised that it is utterly central to the book, because one's intimate relationship can make or break an artist. Your relationship encompasses everything – what you dare to dream, how you deal with money, how you feel about the good times, how you keep going during the bad times, *if* you keep going . . . just about every aspect of being an artist. As author Alison Owings said, 'If my husband hadn't been encouraging I would *either* have written the book, or stayed with him, but I couldn't have done both.'

This chapter is about how to recognise and avoid those people who *say* they do, but clearly do not, love you. And how to teach those who *do* love you, but perhaps don't understand the enormity of your endeavour (or are afraid that if you get too successful you will leave them), to, if not actively help you, to at least stand back and let you do your thing. It is *also* about how to be there for your friends and family who are dealing with the difficult problem of living with *you*. But don't worry, we'll *start* with you.

Writer Virginia Woolf summed up in her journal the impact of a supportive partner perfectly: 'The miracle is accomplished. Leonard put down the last sheet about twelve last night; and could not speak. He was in tears. He says it is "a most remarkable book". He likes it better than *The Wives* . . . I as a witness, not only to his emotion but to his absorption, for he read on and on, can't doubt his opinion: what about my own? Anyhow, the relief was divine.'

When I was married to my first husband, I decided to go back to college and study for my O levels. Our next-door neighbour took care of my son during the day while I attended the local college. But my husband, who was initially proud of me going back to school, became increasingly threatened by it, doing everything in his power to sabotage me. Somehow I managed to pass my O levels anyway, and by the time I was eighteen, I had left him, taking my two-year-old with me.

Over the next few years I had time off from my studies here and there but at twenty-two I went back to college and did my A levels. During exam time my house-mate Simon took over all the cooking and cleaning for six weeks. I know I wouldn't have done so well if he had not been there during that time. I finally went to university – which simply wouldn't have been possible had I stayed with my husband. It was tough doing everything and being a single parent, but it was a hell of a lot easier than dealing with the dead weight of a husband who wanted to hold me back.

In fact, in pretty much any endeavour – from learning another language to painting the ceiling of the Sistine Chapel – it is better to have *no-one* than to have someone in the background putting you down. When Simon Robinson was working in a very difficult job, at which he had to endure a lot of knocks from the outside world, his wife Robyn's support kept him going when he might have given up. 'She was amazing,' he says. 'She was able to cope with me coming home and going nuts, venting frustration and talking about certain people. And she was always totally understanding and supportive, keeping me focused on the importance of the work [creating strategies for language revitalization among aboriginal groups in Canada] rather than on the nature of the work.'

When you are an artist, the stakes are even higher, because you *are* what you do, probably more than in any other profession. Your chosen art is (or should be) the naked expression of your essential self. Therefore any discouragement is going to be doubly undermining; the very essence of soul-destroying. Since your soul is what fuels your creative expression, you must guard against this at all costs.

Think about the words 'encourage' and 'discourage' for a moment. To *en*-courage somebody means to inspire them with courage: to put courage inside them. To *dis*-courage them is to take away their courage. Deciding to devote your life to painting/photography/music/poetry/writing takes every ounce of courage you've got. As Alison says: 'You have enough trouble convincing *yourself* (let alone the rest of the world) you can do it, you shouldn't have to convince your partner too!'

When I was interviewed on *The Russell Davies Show* on Radio 2, he played the boxer's song 'Stand Up and Fight' from one of my favourite movies, *Carmen Jones*, which I'd told him my mother and I had loved when I was a child. I thought it was a bit of a strange choice but afterwards my mother pointed out that it was perfect because the stamina required of a singer (or writer/painter/musician) is the same as that required of a fighter. '. . . until you hear that bell, that final bell, stand up and fight like *hell*.' In the arts, where your success is dependent on other people's tastes, you get knocked down, and have to get back up – again and again.

So when you sink back into your corner you need someone there to rub your shoulders and pour water on you; someone who, because they have made you the object of their utter undivided attention for the duration of the fight, can give you tips about your opponent's weak points, advise you when to jab with your left or right, tell you what you're doing right, inspire you to 'get back in the ring' for another round. This is not the time or place for a demoralising critique about how you're never going to make it and you might as well give up now.

Anyone who has had a personal trainer knows that having someone focused on your progress (as opposed to your mistakes) will inspire you to do things that you simply couldn't do on your own. Remember Sarah Litvinoff who, when I started out as a writer, used to let me read my articles to her over the telephone one paragraph at a time. She never once said, 'I think it would be better if you . . .' She *only* said: 'Oh, it's wonderful, I can't wait to hear the next paragraph! Please call me again as soon as it's done.' She made me keep going. She inspired me to write. And the more I wrote, the better I got at it.

The endurance aspect of the artistic process (see Chapter Four: The Long and Winding Road) relies heavily on being inspired. If someone is killing that inspiration with faint praise, criticism or even by ignoring your creative work, it's harder to keep going. I used to teach a little girl to read after school. It was like pulling teeth. She was inattentive, bored, impossible. But one day she showed me her cartwheels (which she was *really* good at) and her excitement at my enthusiasm really brought home to me that the things we are best at are the things that the world reflects back to us that we can do. If you feel you are no good, it's just human nature to not feel like practising, which means – of course – you won't get better at it.

THE POWER OF TWO

I will listen to anyone's convictions,
but pray keep your doubts to yourself.
Goethe

Two sets of oars, if they're both pulling in the same direction,
are always going to be better than one. 'He supported me in
being fearless, and I gave him discipline,' says Naima Hassan of
her comedy partner and husband Steve Epstein. Simon and
Robyn Robinson are now partners in a design firm that makes
seventeenth-century revivalist paper craft mirrors. 'We auto-
matically fit together because we have different levels of interest
and patience with different parts of the work,' says Simon. 'We
pick up each other's slack.'

'What he does for me is encourage me when I feel down,'
says saxophonist-singer Sheila Cooper, of her husband Andy
Middleton – also a saxophone player. 'He comes to all my gigs.
If I say I don't know if I should invest money in a project he
always tells me I should. He pushes me along when I am fearful.
He believes in me when I falter and don't believe in myself.' And
it works both ways, although Sheila sees her role as slightly
different. 'I remind him how great he is and point out that his
accomplishments mean he should be asking for more money or
doing better projects or whatever,' she says. 'Lady Macbeth-ish,
but without the murder and mayhem.'

They also co-produce each other's CDs, spending the
requisite number of hours (and *hours*) helping to choose the
best cuts and put them in the right order. They both know how
lucky they are. 'It is so hard to have no-one in your corner with
you,' says Sheila, who remembers how it was before they met.

Even when you're in totally different fields, your partner's
support is imperative. Carol Hall was lucky enough to have the

support of her first husband when she started out. 'I had no job skills. I was a wife and mother and worked as a secretary. We didn't have much money so I said I would go and get a job and to his credit he said, "No, you want to be a songwriter. Stay home and write songs."' It allowed her a freedom she would not otherwise have had, as well as showed his belief in her.

'He has faith in me. He loves what I write. He always says, with great admiration, "You've chosen difficult things to write about." And I think, "Oh, good for me!"' says author Alison Owings, about her husband Jonathan. 'I can talk through my ideas with him and I know he will never put them down. It isn't that I am doing it to please him. He thinks I am a serious person and a good writer, and it makes me feel like I *am* a serious person and a good writer because I trust him.'

That trust we have for our intimate partner is similar to the trust we had in our parents (whether misplaced or not) as children. When Marie, an illustrator, was a child her mother often criticised her doing the things that she was good at herself, for example, cooking. 'She would put me down in the kitchen and say I'd never be a good cook,' says Marie. 'But one day, when I was about ten, she said, "You know, you really *are* good at drawing!" And what did I end up doing? It's so basic. What do I do well at and what do I do badly at?' says Marie. 'Well, what my Mama told me when I was ten.'

An intimate partner's love can be as affecting, since there is an element of parent-child intimacy between lovers. 'You are vulnerable. You are naked with them, in both senses of the word. Unprotected. That is what intimacy means,' says Marie, who is lucky enough to 'take for granted' her husband's good faith and belief in her ability. 'You are skinless almost.' It's a big responsibility.

HOT TIP

Remember to love your partner. Thank them for their help. Do things for *them*. It is very easy to be selfish as an artist. Your work (i.e., self-expression) is so all-consuming. Pay attention to them. What do they need? A massage? A day out with you (when you *don't* talk about your work, or go off on a jealous rant about someone who is doing better than you)? Ask them what they need, and give it to them.

SHOULD I STAY OR SHOULD I GO

Friends can help each other. A true friend is someone
who lets you have total freedom to be yourself –
and especially to feel. Or, not feel. Whatever you happen to be
feeling at the moment is fine with them.
That's what real love amounts to –
letting a person be what he really is.

Jim Morrison

Jane's boyfriend, Will, was constantly nit-picking at her achievements. For example, a rave review in a small publication of her first gallery exhibition was dismissed because '. . . it [wasn't] the *New York Times*.' Of course, it is quite possible that what Will was doing was expressing his genuine disappointment on her behalf. But, in that case a simple, 'Wow, darling! I can't wait until you're reviewed by the *New York Times,* too!' would have given the same message. 'As it is, the put-down distracted me from focusing on what I *had* got – an affirmation of my talent, never mind *where* it appeared. These small reviews were the driftwood I clung to while waiting for the hoped-for cruise ship of the *New York Times* to come by and pick me up,' says Jane. 'When he snatched those away from me I felt unsupported, floundering in the water.'

Jane dealt with the issue by communicating directly with him how it affected her and what she wanted instead. And he cared enough about her to pay attention. 'The discussion also brought us closer together because it gave him the chance to explain to me that I can be very needy around my work,' she says. The highs are higher and the lows are lower in the life of an artist, which may make it harder to stick with each other 'for better or for worse', but that's what you both signed up for. 'I realised I was treating him as a cheerleader rather than a boyfriend – expecting him to pick me up all the time.' Communication is key. By addressing their issues directly Will and Jane came to an understanding of each other that helped them both.

Damien was happily married until he decided to pursue his dream to be a music producer. 'When you meet, you believe in each other's dreams, but then a major question becomes, how much are you willing to sacrifice for those dreams,' he says. His wife, Sara, wanted him to give up producing – which was paying him very little money – and get a full-time job that paid well. 'It was like she was saying to me, "Stop being who you are,"' he says. 'I would have been miserable if I'd just taken any old job, but that's what she wanted from me. It was like she had no faith in me that my dream would come true.' It undermined his own faith in that possibility. 'I felt like saying, "Hey, remember me? I'm the guy you fell in love with, and now you want me to be someone else to pay the bills."'

If a person who professes to love you is consistently undermining, in spite of your asking them to stop, you may have to consider removing them from your life. Don't be tempted to keep them around to 'win them over'. Indeed, if you find yourself continuing to engage with them despite the bad effect it has on your work, you might ask yourself if it is merely an act of self-sabotage that you continue to stick around. There are those who manage to be creative in spite of their partner's discouragement. Some, like my friend Miranda, whose husband (now her ex) never read her novel, can even incorporate it into their work. 'I used it as material for my book,' she says. But you should never have to put up with abusive behaviour. What you're doing is hard enough already.

I stayed much longer than I should have in a subsequent relationship with someone who gave me mixed messages all the time. He bought me a microphone and asked me to sing to him in the house. But when I confided that I wanted to do it professionally and dared to compare myself to Alison Moyet, he said: 'How dare you suggest you're as good as Alison Moyet! She's a professional singer! Who the hell do you think you are?' In other words, saying out loud the script that I was already playing in my head all the time anyway. It doesn't take much to suppress a dream that hasn't been born yet.

His intermittent smashing up of my fragile artistic confidence was all the excuse I needed to give up before I began. But, in the end, that was my responsibility. As Eleanor Roosevelt once said, 'No-one can make you feel inferior without your consent.'

When Dolores met Kevin – an aspiring magazine writer – she was working a full-time job and writing on the side. Within a few months of their meeting she landed a book deal for a popular psychology book. 'I was terrified. It was my first book and I had no idea how to write one,' she says. 'So I went to Kevin and said, "Look, can I talk to you. I'm so nervous." I just wanted him to say, "It'll be all right" or something. But he said, "I think we've talked quite enough about your book and I don't want to talk about it ever again."'

He sabotaged her writing at every turn — engineering arguments, putting her down about everything from her looks to her mind. 'You waste so much strength just fighting back or worrying about it,' says Dolores. 'I felt various responses from "Screw you!" to, in my darkest moments, "Maybe I shouldn't be doing this at all." That's not good. Your business as a partner is to support someone doing their thing.' When she left him to live alone, she found she had a lot more energy. 'My ideas had just dried up while we were together. But after I left I dreamed up and sold a new project and it was so much easier without someone in the background saying: "Oh that isn't a very good idea!" all the time.'

Erik, an investment banker turned singer-songwriter, was forced by his ex-girlfriend to choose between her or his music. 'She was jealous about the songs I'd written before we met. Some of them were about my ex-wife and my marriage and she couldn't understand that by now they weren't about that any more. She also hated that I had a passion that was separate from her.' He chose music. 'There are hundreds, fifties and zeros,' says Erik. 'The zeros are the people that discourage you. The fifties like what you do but they don't really get it. And the hundreds, they *get* it!' His current girlfriend is a hundred. 'She almost is in awe of my music,' says Erik. 'It is totally inspiring.'

HOT TIP
Relationships are mirrors. If your partner is not mirroring back a positive image to you, maybe you should leave. If, however, most of your friends are mirroring back the same image, perhaps you need to take a good hard look at yourself.

LET THERE BE LOVE

Lots of people want to ride with you in the limo,
but what you want is someone who will take the bus with you
when the limo breaks down.

Oprah Winfrey

Stability in your relationship is also paramount, since most artistic careers are inherently unstable. Joseph Hooper, a successful magazine journalist for US *Elle*, among others, has been happily married for eighteen years. His wife doesn't particularly involve herself in his career. However, the fact that they have a happy relationship, he says, has affected his career in a positive way. 'It provided me with an emotional stability which gave me the luxury of never having to worry about my relationship,' he says. 'Obviously a good marriage requires work on both sides, but because it was manifestly worth doing, it did provide a good foundation on which to do something other with my life than worry about "will I find love?" or "will my love leave me?"'

Nancy Olewine took on the job of helping her partner, jazz tuba player Howard Johnson, with the business side of his career quite soon after they met. 'Any relationship has to offer you something more than you'd get by being on your own,' she says. Nancy sends out press kits to get work for Howard, who is very appreciative and tells her that it's made a big difference having her support. 'Anybody thrives if they have someone who believes in them,' she says. 'If you support and believe in someone, it does wonders. You don't need to do anything else. I totally respect his abilities and what he's doing. If I couldn't be encouraging, I'd leave. If you're *dis*couraging you're taking a little bit of someone's soul.'

Being believed in is inspiring and supportive. When I was a

child my brother Simon and I wrote plays and short stories and made music together. He would play the guitar and I would sing. When I first started singing to friends, it helped me to have my brother in the room just because I knew that he thought I was a good singer. I have taken that belief with me into adulthood. I don't need my brother to be there in the room any more, but he is somewhere inside me. I have internalised his belief in me.

When I eventually started singing in public, it was at the insistence of my old boyfriend, Mark Burford, who almost had to bully me into doing it – even though it was something I'd yearned to do since I was six years old. However, I had buried my childhood dream until I almost didn't know it was there. I sang for friends sometimes, but I didn't take it seriously. However, after Mark heard me singing around the house he made it his mission not to rest until he'd got me up on to a stage. It was almost as if he pulled it out of me, like a midwife at a difficult birth. I would never have become a singer if I hadn't met him.

As Henry Miller said: 'What sustains the artist is the look of love in the eyes of the beholder. Not money, not the right connections, not exhibitions, not flattering reviews.' Mark made me believe in myself and in the *possibility*. He made me take myself seriously. He'd come to hear other singers with me and encourage me when I felt intimidated. Even as we were breaking up, I used to find little notes pressed in books, or under piles of papers, on which he'd written the titles of songs he thought would be good for me. He would tell me I was as good as Nancy Wilson and other singers I admired. Okay, so it was just his opinion, but I loved him and *respected* his opinion. He 'got it', as Erik would say.

But it is important to realise that playing the supportive role isn't always easy. 'Writers are like vampires. They prey on other people for their inspiration. And they suck the ones they love dry,' acknowledges Veronica Henry. 'And the people that have to suffer for this are my loved ones. Constant reassurance is needed, bolstering, pep talks, practical support and fort-holding. It's too boring for words. It's totally unfair,' she says. 'I would dearly love to be able to handle it on my own, but I can't. My husband is a vital part of the whole process. He's probably suffered more for my art than I have.'

I'm afraid her husband, Peter Bright, agrees. 'Partners supporting, being the kind ear, the psychotherapists, the ego massager, the iron fist, dealing with their rivals, being their knight in shining armour, deserve a medal, we have to put up with a lot of crap – we want to *love you*, not be the whipping boy – that is the price of creativity.' However, Veronica is correct to suspect that he 'secretly' likes it. 'The reason we stick round is that we realise you do need our love. But also, being with a creative woman is all so exciting, unpredictable and very scary,' he says.

Being a creative person's partner requires enormous patience and understanding. When dentist and best-selling novelist Alaa El Aswany was writing *The Yacoubian Building*, he worked twelve hours a day as a Cairo dentist, and then stayed at his office to write in the evenings. Even worse, he spent the weekends in Alexandria, 'to have my solitude and work on the book.' When, after four months of this, his wife asked to see what he'd done, he had only two pages to show for it. 'She was astonished,' he says. 'But I told her I was developing the characters and working in my imagination as well as doing the writing and she was very understanding. She could have thought that I was seeing other women or just having fun but she trusted me.'

And countless artists have been actively assisted by spouses or family members. Nabokov, for example, was married to his stenographer. TS Eliot married his secretary. Simone De Beauvoir edited Jean Paul Sartre's work. Singer Jon Lucien is managed by his wife, Delesa. There are days when I would love someone to come in and just take over and do everything for me, or even run an errand. When my niece stayed with me at a particular crunch period when I was freelance editing a golfing magazine from home, she transcribed interviews for me, made photocopies, cooked in the evenings, did the grocery shopping, stood on line at the post office and – even better – was a fabulous sounding board when I would call out to her, 'What do you think of my opening paragraph?' *And* she wrote some of the articles – although under her own name. I don't know how I managed to stop myself from barring the door when it was time for her to go home.

YOU'VE GOT A FRIEND

> Friendship is the hardest thing in the world to explain. It's not something you learn in school. But if you haven't learned the meaning of friendship, you really haven't learned anything.
> *Muhammad Ali*

By now, if you're single, you might be feeling a bit depressed, or you're focusing on the negative examples of relationships in this chapter. However, your cheerleader doesn't have to be an intimate partner. Vincent Van Gogh had his brother Theo, who sent him money, believed in him, and was almost as focused on Vincent's painting as he was himself. Phoebe, who was in a relationship with someone discouraging, hired a life coach. 'When I realised I wasn't going to get that kind of support at home I thought, "Okay, I'll buy it!"' she says. 'I look on my coach as a wife, a partner, an unconditionally supportive spouse.'

When I decided to make the transition from writing to singing I was lucky enough to have life coach Mark Forster's weekly encouragement for a year. Some of his tips are interspersed throughout this book. He was my sounding board, my confidant, my advisor. I remember describing the experience of being coached by him as like being steered – with Mark as the driver making slight adjustments here and there, talking me through scenarios, helping me to define and refine my goals.

HOT TIP
Consider getting a life coach. Check the Internet for an accredited coach or ask around for a personal recommendation from friends. Take advantage of the free first session many coaches offer, to see if you have good chemistry. You may have to try a few before you settle down. The same applies to choosing from among your friends who to co-coach with.

And if you can't afford a life coach, you can get a friend to co-coach with you. I did that very successfully. We'd make a weekly appointment to fix goals and discuss progress – writing down each other's tasks for the week and holding each other to them. Just having someone totally concentrated on you for one hour a week really helps you to focus yourself.

And, finally, don't forget to just *be* a friend. I used to 'joke' (cough!) that the only reason I became a singer was so I could sing the vocal exercise 'Me! Me! Me! Me! Me!' every day. But I must confess that . . . well, many a true word spoken in jest. About two years into my singing career I woke up one day and realised that I only saw my friends when I was performing. They had almost been reduced in my mind to 'bums on seats'. It's great to have the support and love of your friends, but remember they are your friends, not your 'fans'. Involve yourself in their interests. Spend time with them and don't talk about your career.

It is easy to become obsessed with your work. It is even

necessary. But don't take it too far. Before I became a singer I once heard about a famous opera singer who insisted on having sterilised cups in the dressing room and would send them back if they weren't plastic wrapped. And she went everywhere with a scarf wrapped around her neck, winter and summer. I laughed. But once I started singing regularly I'd think nothing of calling ahead (on the rare occasions I even *went* to non-music-related social gatherings) to see if anyone had a cold. And I'd cancel if they did. Terrible but true. It's a testament to my friends that they stuck around until I came out of it.

And when you find a true friend who really cares about your creative growth, thank your lucky stars. My very wise and life-experienced friend Mansur, who also happens to be the best singer I have ever known, hears all my arrangements, compositions and lyrics before anyone else. He has counselled me through envy and jealousy – my own as well as other people's. He talks me down when I get into a panic about my failures (or successes!). I speak to him at least once a day. I even have his permission to call him at two o' clock in the morning if I need to – and, believe me, I have! And he has come to countless performances of mine and given important feedback. But, most of all, he is a *constant* source of encouragement.

'Keith is the first person to hear my early songwriting efforts,' writes Sting in his memoir, *Broken Music*. 'And although they are probably awful, he shows just enough interest to encourage me to carry on . . . . Maybe all it takes is just one person to believe in what you are doing to give you the confidence to keep trying.'

How you can do it, too

1.   Communicate. Communicate. Communicate. If you don't like something, say so. If you do like something, say so. If

you are unable to communicate your needs without it degenerating into a fight, then invest in a few professional counselling sessions.

2. Periodically ask yourself if you are asking too much of your friends. It's one thing to be self-absorbed, but it is not acceptable to be selfish. There's a difference.

3. If you suspect your partner is deliberately sabotaging you, don't engage with it in the moment. Instead of defending yourself, cut them short with: 'Stop putting me down!' A clear statement of the fact of the put-down, rather than a long-winded explanation as to why it hurts, is far more effective, according to Patricia Evans, author of *The Verbally Abusive Relationship*. Later you can take them aside and make a clear request that they change their behaviour in future. If they won't, then you may have to leave them.

4. Remember to keep a balance between your intimate relationship and your work. Check in with yourself weekly to make sure you are paying enough attention to both. It's very easy to become obsessed with your work. Use your relationship to ground you in your career, and vice versa. Balance is everything.

5. Accentuate the positive. Focus on what you do get. Don't be all doom and gloom about what you are *not* getting from your friends and family. Consider the possibility that they are offering constructive feedback, rather than putting down your achievements. Mark used to tell me off for being self-effacing when presenting myself on stage as 'just Tessa from Cornwall'. I cringed when he pointed it out, but it was true.

6. Make your partner part of your creative life. Make sure they know you value their opinion. Don't alienate them by telling them that they don't understand you and that only another poet/singer/painter/writer could possibly understand.

7.   Be sensitive to your partner. Are you being a drag, grizzling and complaining about how hard it is to be a struggling artist – or, even worse, going on about how great and what a fabulous success you are and how much everyone *else* loves you.

8.   Be careful what you wish for. The last thing you want is a stage mum, living their artistic life vicariously through you. Jenny's husband bullied her about her writing while at the same time not helping around the house or sharing the childcare. All it did was make her feel inadequate and undermined.

You will find as you look back upon your life
that the moments when you have truly lived
are the moments when you have done things in the spirit of love.
Henry Drummond

Chapter Six:
Help! I Need Somebody:
Agents, Managers and Mentors

A good manager can steer you to the greatest heights of success.
A bad manager can be the cause of your career's demise
in no time flat.
Daylle Deanna Schwartz, The Real Deal:
How To Get Signed To a Record Label from A to Z

A manager, agent, mentor, or whatever it is you need at this stage in your career, can make all the difference in getting you to the next level – let alone 'to the greatest heights of success'. But getting representation isn't easy. This chapter will show you the best ways to go about getting this all-important person involved in your career. Before you even begin, it is important to be realistic about where you are now – as opposed to where you think you should be – in order to ascertain which of these, if any, you need. If you are at a very early stage, you are unlikely to require, let alone be able to acquire, representation. But a mentor may be within reach. Or it may be that a friend who is just a little higher up the career ladder than you would be help enough. Or perhaps you need a good teacher in your field. Alternatively, you may want to hire a life coach (see Chapter Five: Love Me or Leave Me).

The main thing is to have someone in your field who can help you get to the next level, who can provide you with an outsider's perspective of what is a realistic next step for you, and help you plan your next moves – much like a boxer having a trainer in his or her corner. Should that person also have better connections than you – as in, for example, an entertainment manager or literary agent – all the better. In the literary world you'll be very lucky even to get your manuscript looked at without an agent who has established connections. In the entertainment world, simply having an enthusiastic champion can get you further than you might imagine.

When I first began to (intermittently) take myself seriously as a singer, my idea of a manager was something like a stage mum. He or she would battle on my behalf; persuade people who needed to be persuaded that I was some kind of musical genius (so I wouldn't have to be immodest), help me create a press kit, assist me in choosing my outfit for performances, introduce me to the 'right' people, including top musicians, book club gigs for me, help me fill the room with cheering fans, talk me up to the press, win back the interest of the first label who had approached me (whom I had mishandled through ignorance and hubris), or – failing that – get me a record deal with someone else. These are all things I would at least attempt to do for my artist if *I* were a manager. And having someone batting for you always makes people think that you're something special.

So when I got management I thought, 'Hooray! Now all my troubles are over. Success is imminent!' However, although I have had not one but two managers in my short career, neither of them did any of the above on my behalf. Because they weren't that kind of manager and I didn't take the trouble to find out what kind of managers they were. I was also somewhat blinded by the light of the stars (granted, no-one that major, but definitely more major than I was) already on their roster. I was only a couple of years into my singing career when I got involved with them, and knew next to nothing about the industry, I was also extremely naïve. I loved music. I had faith in my ability and talent. I felt I had a shot at some kind of success. And I hadn't heard the Hunter S. Thompson pronouncement that: 'The music business is a cruel and shallow money trench, a long plastic hallway where thieves and pimps run free, and good men die like dogs. There's also a negative side.'

That's not to say that either of my managers were thieves or pimps. Looking back I realise they both meant well. Indeed, both helped me considerably on my first CD – one by loaning me the money to get the master out of studio hock and spending an afternoon in the studio with me, and the other – my former manager – by coming in for a few hours at the last minute to do the final honing of the mix. But they were not managers who did artist development, which is what I needed. And by rights, they should have told me that and turned me down at the beginning. At the end of ten months, the first one had not presented me to one label. After exactly one year, the second one had presented me to one label (within the first month) – who turned me down – and stalled there.

But before I get ahead of myself, I should perhaps begin by telling you how to get representation in the first place.

SOMEONE TO WATCH OVER YOU

The reason Gunnell became my manager is because he was very happy with me packing out the Flamingo.

Georgie Fame

In most cases you will need to work up to getting any form of representation. In other words you must have something to represent, or manage. It is almost unheard of for artists without experience, or at least some professional foothold in the field, to be taken on. Representatives work on commission, not for a salary, and therefore are virtually gambling on your success. It stands to reason that they would prefer to take on a safe bet, i.e. someone who has already proved themselves to some extent.

In fiction, you will find it easier to get an agent if you have graduated from a respected Master of Fine Arts programme, or have had your stories published in literary magazines, or appeared in print somewhere. After one of my humour pieces appeared in New York *Metro* magazine, I was approached by a literary agent who wanted to know if I was working on a novel. I already had an agent, however. In photography it depends on whether you are an arts photographer or journalist. If the former, you will, like any visual artist, have to do the rounds of the galleries. If you are a photojournalist, then pitching story ideas, and showing samples of your work to the photo editors on the publications you are interested in, is par for the course. In all cases you must be the squeaky wheel. When you have some kind of a career to manage, *that* is when you can think about getting a manager.

But, even if you have something to sell, it is important to understand the reality of the marketplace from the get-go, to give you some idea of the enormity of your task. On the other hand, don't be daunted by it. There are always exceptions that prove the rule, and who's to say that it's not you. But it is hard work, for you *and* your representative. For example, in publishing, eighty per cent of the general population thinks they have a book in them. Of that eighty per cent, a small fraction gets agents. And from that fraction, only two per cent will get sold to a publisher. And even after that, only thirty per cent of that two per cent will turn a profit. Newcomers, or non-names, are the hardest sell of all, so it's unlikely that an agent or manager will be willing to take on a total newcomer, unless the agent is incredibly powerful and their name behind the artist is enough to turn heads.

'There are a lot of technically proficient jazz artists out there and for that reason I'm looking for those who have not only talent but something very individual about their music,' said my booking agent Reggie Marshall, when I asked him for some advice for this chapter. 'There has to be something that sets them apart from the pack. And if they're just starting out they have to move me emotionally in a big way for me to make a commitment of my time and energy, given that the financial return on that investment is by no means certain regardless of how good they are.'

Ultimately, if you're an artist just starting out, the right agent for you is the one who feels most strongly about your art and will work hardest for you, because working on your career is a time-intensive endeavour. 'This may not be the most powerful agent, because the bulk of his or her time is of necessity going to go to those artists who are his bread-and-butter clients,' says Reggie. 'He might be excited for a minute and then if he doesn't get an immediate response when he sends out your CD you may be shunted quickly to a rapidly-cooling back burner.'

It is your job, dear reader, to think of what you have in your arsenal to give 'added value' to the (it goes without saying, but I'll say it anyway) very high quality of the work. For example, when twenty-year-old Jane Monheit came second in the highly prestigious Thelonious Monk competition, the resulting publicity got her name out there and she was taken on by a major heavyweight manager who developed her career. Talent alone is not always enough; you have to stand out in some way – either by virtue of your great youth, your great age, a totally unique style (also known as a USP – unique selling point), your insane beauty, your kooky weird clothes, or whatever.

'Having your own voice and your own identity is key,' agrees

Veronica Henry. 'It is inevitable that comparisons are made, because people love to pigeonhole. Because I wrote about the English countryside and my characters behaved rather badly at times I was compared to Jilly Cooper – which I'm sure she found more irritating than I did! After all, she was one of my heroines, one of the writers I devoured and, incidentally, not one who I felt confident I could emulate. But to stand out, you do need to be confident in your own voice, know what sort of story you are trying to tell, and how.'

HOT TIP

When making a pitch to anyone, have a good one- or two-sentence description of yourself that differentiates you from the crowd and is intriguing. For example, I don't say I am a jazz singer (a very broad category). I say, 'My music is definitely jazz, but it has a strong Middle Eastern and Flamenco influence, and I compose a lot of my own songs.'

Whether you are an aspiring singer, writer, actor, or visual artist, the first thing is to go to the Internet, which is a wonderful resource for information on everything, Identify a dozen artists in your field, at your level or a bit above, and figure out who represents them. You may be able to get this information from their web sites, or from the acknowledgements in their books. If you are a writer, it would not be untoward to approach the agent of an author who writes in the same genre as you do, but within that genre you have to differentiate yourself in some way. However, if you are a blonde-haired piano-playing female jazz singer, you don't want to approach Diana Krall's manager. After the success of Norah Jones's first CD, her producer, Arif Mardin, says he was approached by countless Norah Jones sound-a-likes, hoping he would discover them. Of course he wasn't interested, because he already had Norah.

Once you've identified a few agents/managers, start by approaching about ten. Bear in mind that each field will have different requirements. Basically, your job is to present what you do as succinctly as possible. Put together a package containing a query letter and sample chapter, show reel, or other relevant material, which showcases your talent. Include a one-page (max – these people are very busy and will be put off by massive tomes) bio or résumé and a professional head shot, where relevant. A literary agent may not be interested in a bio, or in your appearance, unless you are incredibly beautiful or handsome (à la Sebastian Junger), which they might consider an extra selling point. Your package must be as professional-looking as possible – that means no typos! – and make sure you address it to the correct contact person, and that his or her name is spelled correctly. Agents are so inundated that they are looking for any excuse not to have to examine yet another submission. A misspelling might make the difference between having your package opened or not. If possible, show your package to a knowledgeable friend in your field before you send it.

Don't be afraid to name-drop. When I approached my second manager I called ahead to his secretary, who told me that they weren't looking for any more artists. However, I mentioned my mentor Mark Murphy, and the fact that a major label had expressed an interest in my demo, and she went away and asked the manager if I could send my package. It turned out he was a big fan of Mark Murphy, and I was told I could send in my demo, bio and pictures. I was also told to put a particular codeword on the envelope or it wouldn't even be opened. Use whatever you have in your arsenal to get your work seen or heard. Because you could be the next Eva Cassidy, but it's not going to do you any good if no-one puts your demo on the CD player. In fact, Eva Cassidy was turned down by several major labels when she was alive, who must be kicking themselves now.

Here's where networking can really help. In the arts, in addition to be being talented, knowing the right people opens doors. A mentor, for example, is an established artist in your field who has better connections than you do. The fact that my mentor and teacher was legendary jazz vocalist Mark Murphy introduced me to a lot of people I would not have met otherwise.

So how did I get to Mark in the first place? And more importantly, how could you get a mentor too? I first met him at a jazz vocal workshop he was giving. I sang 'Round Midnight' and thought I'd done a really good job, but afterwards, Mark said to me: 'Now, why did you hold that long note at the end?' and I had to admit that I'd held it to show off how long I could hold a note — the very worst reason on earth. The fact that he'd called me on it made me realise that he was a very good teacher. So when a few months later I got a call from his then assistant saying he had asked if I would run his jazz vocal workshops in exchange for free lessons I jumped at the opportunity. This led to me becoming his quasi-assistant. That I would be doing quite a lot of work in exchange for his mentorship is not that unorthodox. In fact, it placed me in something of a tradition. Playwright Samuel Beckett was James Joyce's secretary. Carmen McRae cleaned house for Billie Holiday.

Being Mark's assistant got my name out there. Very occasionally it worked to my disadvantage, because some people would assume that devoting myself to another singer must mean I couldn't be a good singer myself. But that was only until they heard me. Overall, I would say it did me a lot of good. Musically, it was like putting on seven league boots. But he also advised me on the practicalities of the business. Don't underestimate the value of approaching an artist in your field and asking for their advice, let alone offering your services in exchange for free lessons or coaching. And failing that, find out if any of the artists you love are giving private lessons or teaching classes. Mark has helped many of the singers he teaches to make good connections. Raymond Carver had some of his short stories published with the help of his guru, John Gardner.

But get the right one. Being this kind of teacher or mentor requires great generosity. If the teacher you sign up with only wants to talk about themselves or 'demonstrate' how a song should be sung, rather than help bring out what is already in *you*, they probably shouldn't be teaching. And some excellent singers are poor teachers, just because they aren't experienced. It is the same with writing or painting or any creative discipline. Play the field until you hit on someone who is right for you.

HOT TIP

When seeking a mentor, look around in your field for an artist you really admire and offer your services in return for their mentorship. Be realistic. Clearly, offering to help Jennifer Lopez organise her wardrobe in return for singing lessons isn't going to happen. But non superstars – authors, journalists, photographers, designers and jazz musicians – are surprisingly approachable.

During the two and a half years it took Alaa El Aswany to write *The Yacoubian Building*, his mentor Alaa El Deeb, a literary critic and writer, was reading all his work. 'He still reads all my work,' says Alaa. When he finished the novel, his mentor was the first person he gave it to. 'I went to his house at two a.m. and then my family and I waited for him to give us his opinion. When he called at eight-thirty in the morning, after reading it all night, my family couldn't hear what he was saying while I was on the phone. But when they heard me say, "Thank you very much!" my wife, son and little daughters all burst into applause. He said that he had kept reading it all night and that it was an important work that would make history.'

I can't stress enough how encouraging words like this can be coming from someone you look up to. Legendary tuba player Howard Johnson, who toured with Charles Mingus, arranged for Gil Evans for twenty years, and recorded with many of the giants of jazz, once took me aside after a gig we did together and said, 'Tessa. When are you going to realise that you are an *important* musician?' It was like being given water in the desert. When I am flagging, I take a sip of that remark and it gives me the strength to stagger on for a few more steps. Howard, although not my mentor, definitely has some of those qualities. When we first performed together and my impulse was to ask his opinion about my ideas for how a song should go, he'd put up his hands and say, 'You're the bandleader!' It gave me confidence, just as Mark did every time he gave me positive feedback.

I was with Mark for four years, but a 'mentor' may even be someone that you work with for a matter of weeks. When Jane Lyle got her first book deal she was writing the odd freelance article and working full time as a picture researcher. 'I negotiated a really good advance and I was able to give up my job to write, so at first I was very pleased with myself,' says Jane. 'But when I realised I'd never written a book before I was terrified. I didn't know how to do it at all. I felt sick. I thought I'd have to give all the money back. I used to pace up and down the flat thinking: "I've got to write fifty thousand words and I don't know where to start!" I had no *idea*!'

Luckily, a friend knew a well-known writer who Jane had met once or twice, and she said: 'Listen, why don't you call and ask his advice?' She did. 'He was brilliant. He lent me books and helped me to plan it,' she says. Every week for three weeks she trooped up the stairs to his flat and he coached her through the basic tools of how to do research and draw up a plan. 'It was so helpful. When I left his flat every week I felt totally confident,' says Jane, who has written several best sellers since, including *The Lover's Tarot*, *The Destiny Cup* and *Sacred Sexuality*. When embarking on my career in journalism, starting from scratch with no connections, I appointed journalist and author Sarah Litvinoff, who I had only just met, as a kind of mentor. I used to call her for advice, or ask her to look at my writing. She also introduced me to magazine editors, pumping me up to them in advance.

Composer Carol Hall, who wrote the score for *The Best Little Whorehouse in Texas*, got her start when the great singer Mabel Mercer performed two of her songs (see Chapter One: All You Have To Do Is Dream). 'Everyone used to go to her weekly concert,' says Carol. 'Sinatra used to say he learned everything about phrasing from her. And I'm sure that's where Barbra Streisand heard my song "Jenny Rebecca", which she subsequently recorded.' But the main thing was that the room was full of singers and songwriters and was a marvellous networking opportunity. Getting Mercer's support opened doors. 'You could call someone up and say, "I have two songs being sung by Mabel Mercer." And music people would then accept your package. Obviously from then on you were on your own.'

GETTING TO KNOW YOU

They always say time changes things,
but you actually have to change them yourself.
Andy Warhol

But of course talent and tenacity will more than make up for a lack of connections, and let you forge your own. As nineteenth-century author James Garfield once said, 'A pound of pluck is worth a ton of luck.' When art photographer Michael Becker first got his work into a gallery, he went in cold. 'I went to an art gallery in the town where I used to live and I happened to mention to the owner that I did photography and it might be good for his gallery because I saw he liked pictures of local scenes,' he says. 'He said, "Well I don't do much photography and I get people in here all the time asking if they can exhibit here but you can send me a couple of jpegs if you like." He was very blunt and said he would only put up stuff he was sure would sell. So I did that and he absolutely loved them and offered me a show more or less straightaway.' The show was a great success and Michael was invited back.

Networking is a great way of meeting potentially helpful people. I met my literary agent socially long before she became my agent – not that she was an agent, or I in need of one, at the time. But after she became one I turned to her for advice when the idea for this book came up and then she offered to represent me. Make it your business to meet as many people in your field as you can. Consider joining a writers' group, a small theatre company, or sitting in at jam sessions. Go to art openings, book readings and industry parties. And in every case, don't hesitate to introduce yourself to anyone in the room who appeals to you. I've been known to approach total strangers with the line, 'You look like the most interesting person in the room. I'm going to attach myself to you if you don't mind.'

The same principle of attendance applies to trade events by the way. Almost all industries hold annual trade shows that welcome the public and even hold seminars and panel discussions for aspiring artists in that field. I made the initial contact with my booking agent, Reggie, at the International Annual Jazz Education conference. Of course, it goes without saying that you should look as good as possible without being over the top

– turning up to sing at a jazz jam wearing a glittery silver dress and dragging a fox fur on the ground behind you would be just as bad as turning up at a fashion magazine schmooze looking like a scarecrow.

And as any good boy or girl scout knows, always be prepared. You never know when an opportunity to promote yourself to someone might arise. Dutch singer Fleurine, wife of pianist Brad Meldau, had written lyrics to a Thelonious Monk tune. Getting the Monk estate to hear it would have been a virtual imposs-ibility – they are inundated with requests. However, one day she ran into his son, T.S. Monk, at a music schmoozing event, and she asked him if he would be willing to listen to them. When he said yes, she dashed off to the loo, sang the song with her lyrics into her tape recorder, and gave him the tape. A few months later, he called, giving her permission to record the song. You can even approach the artist directly by going backstage after a performance. That's how I got permission to record my lyrics to guitarist Pat Martino's song 'Willow'.

But impromptu schmoozing opportunities aside, getting a manager or agent or mentor requires setting up a system. Make a chart on which you record who you have approached and when, what you submitted and their response, if any. This is vital when it comes to the next stage – the dreaded follow-up calls. Practically to a man, or woman, no-one I have asked can bear this part of the process. But it has to be done – unless you are very lucky, as I was with my booking agent, who contacted me a few months after he had received my package. I had done no follow-up to the extent that I initially had no idea how he got my demo in the first place, but when I looked at my chart, I saw that I had sent it to him a few months before – for which I patted myself on the back, by the way.

When making follow-up calls, it goes without saying that you should always be polite, friendly and attractive about it. When I was booking the Sweet Rhythm jazz club I was inundated with submissions from singers who wanted to be part of my vocal series. Sometimes they would come to the club and be annoyingly 'hungry' or needy or already acting like it was my life's ambition to reject them. The most effective approaches were those from people who charmingly said they hoped I'd get to listen to their CD because they would 'really value' my opinion. Maybe it appealed to my vanity. Or perhaps it brought out the big sister in me. Whichever. It worked — to the extent that I'd be flung into paroxysms of guilt if I didn't like their CDs.

Be patient, since the person you are approaching may be extremely busy. Don't do what a singer I know did and call and leave a message with a club booker saying, 'How come you have that terrible singer you just hired but you can't get back to me!' Never do this — even if it's how you feel. Perhaps the terrible singer had connections. Or — quite likely — they were more charming than my friend. (By the way, don't make these calls when you are feeling at all bitter and twisted about how hard this business is; they will hear it in your voice.)

If an entertainment manager/agent hasn't done anything significant for you within a year, find out if it is because they just haven't presented you, or if there is a good reason. It is good to talk to your representative in advance to find out if they have a specific time-frame in mind. Something concrete, rather than an airy fairy '. . . oh, a while'. Communication is key, as with any close relationship (see Chapter Five: Love Me or Leave Me). It may be that they've been trying really hard without any success. Most agents will let their clients know promptly if a project doesn't look like it's going to get off the ground, in which case you may want to discuss taking another tack, or parting company. And don't be afraid to leave. A manager who is not working on your behalf is worse than no manager at all.

But it may simply be a time management issue. Because the

fact of the matter is that heavyweight managers, especially those with large client lists, are often too busy with their artists that are already earning them money to devote much time to those who need development. Since, without development, you are unlikely to get to the stage where you will earn them money, you have a bit of a chicken and egg situation – only without the chicken. It would be great if they told you that at the outset. But, to be fair to them, they may not realise. All they know is that they heard something good in you and they want to sign you up just in case. Then they get overwhelmed with their other clients, and forget all about you.

This is entirely understandable. Most managers/agents are in it for the money. And why shouldn't they be? However, most artists, as we have already ascertained, are not in it for the money. Most artists are in it because they can't *not* be in it, which, as I've said, sets up an immediate power imbalance in favour of the managers. If you find a manager/agent who is doing it for love, I'd advise you to cling on for dear life. I knew some-one who was very successfully represented by a friend. And there is a long tradition of spouses handling their partners' careers. However, managers can get burned too, and the few who started out doing it for love have often had their asses kicked somewhere along the way by some success-hungry artist who dumped them as soon as they'd got them to a level where they began making money.

Terrible stories abound of artists firing agents and managers by fax or email. If you do decide that it's time for you to part company, treat that person with the same sort of respect that you would give to ending any intimate relationship. Discuss the practicalities of separating. There may be contract issues. Or they may be able to pass you on to a colleague who is less busy.

> **HOT TIP**
> Remember, agents and managers are in it for the money; it's your responsibility to be marketable. To them you are a commodity, however friendly you are with each other. When you get down to the nitty gritty, it's a professional relationship.

WHAT HAVE YOU DONE FOR ME LATELY?

When you're drowning, you don't say, 'I would be incredibly pleased if someone would have the foresight to notice me drowning and come and help me,' you just scream.
John Lennon

Judge any manager/agent on what they do for you and remember that no matter how 'powerful' a manager/agent is, if they have taken you on (thus preventing you from being cared for by anyone else) they owe it to you to do that work on your behalf. And have a time limit in mind. If they don't deliver what they've said they will within a realistic period of time (which you have ascertained with them in advance), move on. Whatever you do, don't do what I did and wake up one morning to realise that yet another year has managed to slip past without my realising, with no activity. At the end of the day, it will look to the outside world as if you are a hard sell and they tried and failed to sell you, rather than that they didn't try at all.

And if you get someone who *is* working hard on your behalf, don't forget who helped you once you get anywhere. Janet, an illustrator, regrets walking away from an agent who she felt was driving her too hard. 'Now I realise I had the wrong attitude,' she says. And one of the best managers I ever witnessed, admittedly from the outside, was completely new to the job, but took on a musician who had been struggling unsuccessfully for twenty years and basically did all the things I describe at the beginning of this chapter that I dreamed a manager would do – including get him into a club that had initially said no, and then personally see to it that the room was filled with friends. Naturally the musician was invited back. However, within a year of that gig, the manager was fired for being 'too interfering'.

Personally I am in favour of talking out issues and staying with the same person for good, as long as they are honourable, and trustworthy. If you catch them acting without integrity, or lying, then of course they must be tossed aside like a bad boyfriend – although I would counsel against bad-mouthing them after-wards. But, apart from that, you should expect to grow together and make mistakes together. No-one is perfect and no-one can know everything. You don't just do a runner when someone better-looking turns up. You address what is missing in your current relationship. It's not that different from a marriage, or any long-term relationship. Speaking of which, make sure you get a contract or something written down so that you are both clear on what to expect of each other and how each gets paid. Agents and managers work on commission. If anyone asks for a salary, or any kind of upfront payment, run.

Managers and agents help those who help themselves – as long as you're not interfering. When I subsequently got taken on by my booking agent, Reggie, with whom I'm very happy, I made sure that I kept myself uppermost in his mind – sending him leads, notes on how to sell me, and asking his advice about what to do next. I discuss with him at every turn any question that comes to mind. When at the beginning of our relationship he was having trouble getting me big-paying gigs, I called a meeting in which I asked him what he thought the problem was.

At the end of that meeting we decided that he should help me with career-building, booking me lower-paying gigs until I was more established, and concentrating our efforts on getting a recording deal with distribution to help establish me.

The tone of our relationship was set from the very start. When we first decided to work together, I met him to discuss business. At that first meeting, we both talked about our previous experiences and what we expected of each other. I feel his support and belief in me, even on this book (he used to be a screenwriter), and he keeps me real and sensible in my music career expectations. He sends me positive feedback he receives on me, and if someone doesn't like my style, he reminds me that this is an industry driven by personal taste. 'I mean, *I* love your music, Tessa, but not everyone will,' he once said to me, which totally stopped me in my tracks because, strangely, it hadn't occurred to me before. Having him in my corner has made all the difference to how I cope with the business emotionally, as well as on a professional level. And having him chase after gigs for me gives me time to focus on my music, *and* spares me from the stress of having to deal with overwhelmed and overworked club owners and festival presenters myself.

Remember, just as in a marriage, you won't always agree, but you can resolve your issues. Bullying, threats, emotional blackmail or power struggles from either side are not to be tolerated. Frequent communication is vital. As America's most famous advice columnist Ann Landers once said, 'All married couples should learn the art of battle as they should learn the art of making love. Good battle is objective and honest – never vicious or cruel. Good battle is healthy and constructive, and brings to a marriage the principle of equal partnership.' And that is what we are talking about here – a partnership. In the best case scenario, a manager or agent, mentor or teacher relationship will benefit you both.

As Carl Jung said: 'The meeting of two personalities is like the contact of two chemical substances: if there is any reaction, both are transformed.' It is up to you to make sure that this transformation is for the better.

How you can do it, too

1. Make a realistic assessment of your present career level and of where you want to end up. Then decide what your next step should be. That will help you ascertain whether you need a manager, a mentor, a booking agent, additional professional training, or even a life coach.
2. Read up on your industry. Libraries are full of books on finding an entertainment or literary agent, a music manager, a record label, etc. Have realistic expectations about what professional help can do for you.
3. Network. Never underestimate the power of schmoozing. You have to create a buzz about yourself, and the more people who have heard of you, the more likely it's going to happen. A lot of jazz gigs are got through people hearing you sit in at jam sessions. Get yourself invited to and then attend all the industry parties that you can bear. Count it as part of your job. Once there, introduce yourself to as many people as possible, taking care not to be rudely looking over their shoulder to see if anyone more interesting just walked in.
4. Have something to manage/handle. You can't just turn up with a dream. You need to prove you can have a career, by showing that you have a body of work.
5. Don't necessarily assume that only a big wheel can handle your career. Singer Jon Lucien is handled very successfully by his wife. Filmmaker David Munro married his producer, Xandra Castleton.

6. When approaching an agent, position yourself as different from the other artists that the agent already represents: Two Norah Joneses in one manager's stable would be one too many. But a Diana Krall and a Norah Jones in the same stable makes perfect sense.

7. If, when you meet your potential agent or manager, you come away with their entire life story – especially if that involves a lot of self-important name-dropping – take that as a warning sign that they are probably more interested in themselves than they will ever be in you.

8. Ask around about particular managers in advance of signing anything. Don't expect to get the truth about what people really think of your manager once you are signed to them. The arts industry is a small world and people will fear things getting back.

9. Get a contract, and don't be afraid to walk away if it doesn't give you what you need. Show any contract to a good entertainment lawyer who can look it over with you. Don't feel this is getting too big for your boots, or going behind your potential manager's back. It's merely good sense, and it will show them you're not a pushover.

10. You need a manager who is willing to work with you at your level. A manager or agent who has a massive or star-studded client list is probably going to be too busy to focus on you, especially if their other artists are already making them money. It goes almost without saying that they must love and believe in your work.

11. Managers help clients who help themselves. Don't give up all responsibility for your career: if someone else is taking care of your career, make sure they *are*. Arrange periodic meetings to discuss development.

12. Once you have a manager, don't be afraid to ask questions. I *should* have asked all of the following of my managers.

When will you send my demo and package around to labels? Who were you thinking of targeting and why? When would you expect something – if anything – to happen? What do you think is my next step? How can we get my career to the next level? What do you need from me that will make your job easier? Why haven't you done anything so far?

13. Once you have an agent or manager, if at any point you feel you are not moving forward, call a meeting, having first written out for yourself (so you can get it really clear in your head) what you want to achieve in your career within a certain time-frame.

14. Agents, managers and mentors are all there to help introduce you to a higher level of professional contacts. The right manager or agent should be in a position to get you and/or your work seen or heard by the right person. Because in the arts, it's all about taste, and getting the right person in the right place to like what you do, and put it out there and promote it.

15. Artists are notoriously bad at handling the money side of their careers. Just remember, the more you delegate responsibility, the more vulnerable you are to those forces that would take advantage of you (see Chapter Three: I Will Survive). In a good artist agreement, these issues will be outlined to the nth degree in very simple language.

I had a sports coach when I was a child who always said, 'He can, who thinks he can.' It stayed with me to this day.
Freddy Cole

Chapter Seven: Helter Skelter: Handling the Emotional Roller Coaster of the Artist's Life

I don't know what other singers feel when they articulate lyrics, but being an eighteen-carat manic-depressive and having lived a life of violent emotional contradiction, I have an over-acute capacity for sadness as well as elation . . . I've been there and back. I guess the audience feels it along with me.

Frank Sinatra

Following your creative dream can be so wearing at times — financially, emotionally, spiritually — that depression is almost guaranteed. Of course being creative has its wonderful *moments* (mainly when you are actually practising your craft), or we wouldn't do it at all. But periods of elation followed by periods, just as long if not longer, of feeling in the depths of despair, can leave you as emotionally exhausted as if you just got off a ten-hour roller coaster ride. Countless artists simply give up, either by actually giving up or, even worse, resorting to the reckless abuse of drugs or by committing suicide.

This is not to say, of course, that all artists are potential manic depressives running around with hypodermic needles sticking out of their arms. But the necessary dredging up of the inner-most depths of your being that goes with the territory of being creative *hurts*. Dr Keith Simonton, a professor of psychology at the University of California, Davis, who has studied the high suicide rate among poets, posits: 'It could be that people are using poetry as a form of self-therapy.' And, as the saying goes, 'a little knowledge is a dangerous thing'.

I used to assume that the suffering was due to the fact that artists are more sensitive souls than non-artists. Or perhaps it's the lifestyle that goes with being an artist. As Henry Miller said, 'What is an artist's life? Depression and poverty.' Whatever the reasons behind it, I now realise that however well-balanced you are when you start out, you are unlikely to get very far into pursuing your chosen art form without having to negotiate your way through the mood swings, super highs and down-in-the-depths lows, self-doubts and fears and deep depressions that are part and parcel of most artists' lives.

In fact, depression is so synonymous with the artistic sensibility that most people have come to believe that it is not possible to be a 'true artist' without also being a depressive. Artists are just more delicate souls, people assume. Who else but an artist would get depressed when things are going *well*? Add to that the feeling of powerlessness that goes with being in a profession where whether you succeed or fail depends on other people's opinions and tastes and you've got a recipe for disaster.

This chapter is about how to ride the tumultuous waves of this life you have chosen and get yourself onto a more even keel. The mood swings, caused by the successes and the failures, the unexpected lows when things are going well, the verging on manic highs when things are good, the prolonged periods of workaholism followed by 'fallow' periods of relative inactivity or feelings of hopelessness. Obviously this chapter cannot be a substitute for therapy from a trained psychologist, but I hope that my experiences and those of others in this chapter will help you to identify and cope with some of the emotional issues that you will encounter that are specific to being a creative person.

HOT TIP
Understand that ups and downs are par for the course. You may be feeling down now, but later on, you *will* feel up. Just look back at your past and remember the last two times you felt wonderful and the last two times you felt terrible about your career. Write them down. If *only* life were a series of ever increasing joys. Then again, if it were, would we really appreciate the highs if we didn't have periods of suffering to compare them with? Maybe not.

THINGS FALL APART

Along with success come drugs, divorce, fornication, bullying, depression, neurosis and suicide. With failure comes failure.
Joseph Heller

When I first used to hang out in jazz clubs I was absolutely shocked to find musicians taking drugs – even heroin. The junkie jazz musician is such a cliché that I was amazed that people were still doing it. Now that I've been a musician for a few years, I understand. In fact, I'm more amazed at the number of people who don't do it. It's a hard life. And, although I admit I have suffered from depression on and off from the age of about twelve, since I became a singer (and to a lesser extent when I was a writer) I have definitely suffered higher highs and lower lows than before I started my artistic careers.

'Some days I am all over the place, convinced that I have the hardest job in the world and that no-one else could possibly do it and how on earth can I be expected to dredge up inspiration from nowhere,' says novelist Veronica Henry. 'After a few days of wallowing I have to give myself a stern talking-to and tell myself to get on with it in a professional and objective manner! But the truth is, writing is not like a pile of ironing that you can tackle head-on and plough through till you get to the end. It can take any amount of time for stories, characters, relationships to gel, and it can't be forced. And sometimes you have to do the worst thing and throw everything out. That is seriously hard, but entirely necessary. And, after the initial pain, a huge relief, as you no longer have to do battle with something that isn't working. That's when you can move on. In the meantime . . . The blackness. And the euphoria. Thank God for the euphoria.'

In the 'blackness' I have also discovered and had to face parts of myself I didn't know existed. 'You must be prepared to have the worst in you brought out,' says David Walmer, a Wall Street broker turned singer-songwriter. In my case, along with the good – an aptitude for sewing clothes and designing my own brochures and postcards, the ability to be generous (most of the time), and a willingness to work hard to get to where I am today – I discovered I was also capable of jealousy, pettiness, despondency, hopelessness, neediness, greed, anger, even bitterness. All things I would love to totally disown and blot out of my mind. Luckily I got into the business too old to be taken unawares by the temptation of illegal drugs. But I feel for those who *have* succumbed in order to keep going, as well as for those who have given up the ghost completely. I have considered giving up my craft many, many times, simply because I couldn't handle the mood swings. In fact, I have, in my time, taken anti-depressants.

My depression also prevented me from doing a reality check which affected other areas of my life. When I was broke, part of my problem was refusing to accept that I wasn't making any real money from my art. When I ended up in housing court and had to be bailed out by a friend, it was slammed home to me that I had allowed myself to become dangerously broke. Then I found part-time work. Somehow, living on hope and expectations, and the idea that 'just around the corner' I was going to make money from singing had prevented me from accepting the fact of my 'present' circumstances – and acting on them.

And it's not even about being broke or unacknowledged. The rich/famous/respected are not immune to suffering, either – Dylan Thomas, Virginia Woolf, Jimi Hendrix, Diane Arbus, Benny Hill, Brooke Shields and countless others have suffered from depression. Comedian Rodney Dangerfield, who started writing jokes when he was fifteen, 'to try to escape being unhappy', once said that depression is an occupational hazard of being a comedian. 'The better the comedian, the more depressed he is,' he said. Even Kate Winslet – who has surely been on a career roll since she starred in *Sense and Sensibility* as a teenager – isn't immune. On the set of *Titanic*, she wrote in her journal, 'I feel ugly, talentless and uncommitted, frightened, lonely, nervous, mad, and we haven't started shooting yet.'

At my worst, I stopped listening to music. I was unable to listen to successful singers because I'd get too caught up in the issue of what did they have that I didn't. I couldn't even listen to the radio. I told myself it was because I didn't want to be derivative of other singers, but the truth was, I was jealous (more on this in Chapter Eight). I wouldn't dream of sitting in on a jam session – even though I'd done it all the time before I considered myself a professional – for fear that I'd mess up and look bad in front of other people, completely forgetting that it was supposed to be fun.

And I started to feel bitter about people who were getting good gigs because of who they knew, rather than because of their talent. At the start of my singing career I didn't give a toss, and couldn't understand the people who did. And, of course, being rejected – which is part and parcel of a business where personal taste counts for everything – is always depressing. And no wonder. 'Every secret of a writer's soul, every experience of his life, every quality of his mind is written large in his works,' said Virginia Woolf. It is no less than a rejection of *you*.

'The strange thing about any artistic pursuit is you develop a thick skin,' says actor Graham McTavish. 'You learn to take enormous amounts of rejection that would break some people. And sometimes it does. Sometimes they give up. But you have to ride every single rejection and say, "Oh I'll just get the next job." And you do.' But that's sometimes easier said than done. 'It's the people on the business side of it that depress me,' says singer-saxophonist Sheila Cooper, who was once rejected by a label because, as the A&R person said, 'She's a good singer and saxophone player, but no-one wants to see someone that pretty play the sax.' Ouch!

The *only* way past an experience like that is, not necessarily, as Graham says, to get the next job, but to learn how to handle *not* getting the next job. In my case meditation has been a wonderful tool to help me cope with life as it is, as opposed to how I think it should be, and oddly that in itself seems to make life more likely to flow, and the benefits can spill over into other areas of your life. When I first learned Transcendental Meditation in my twenties, it changed my life almost overnight. Prior to meditating, I would leave the house in the morning and arrive at the bus stop, which would either be completely empty (I'd just missed the bus) or packed with other people. Never mind if I'd been the first person there, by the time the bus arrived, there would be an unruly gaggle of sociopaths karate chopping each other out of the way in their determination to be the only person to get on the overcrowded bus that had taken half an hour to arrive.

If by some stroke of luck I happened to have clawed my way onto the deck, the bus conductor would invariably pronounce that the bus was full and push the excess people (including me) off the bus, leaving an irate rugby scrum of infuriated commuters shouting pathetically after the bus: 'But I was here first!' After learning to meditate, my mind was more focused and less of a jumble. I would leave the house, calmly note the rugby scrum at the bus stop in the distance and, without panicking, reach the near corner of the road just as the bus pulled up at a red light. If the conductor was magically upstairs collecting fares, I would take the opportunity to leap onto the deck and squirm my way to the middle of the bus, where he wouldn't notice me until it was too late. My entire life was easier, because I had learned to slow down my mind and offset the stress that would otherwise overwhelm me.

Another way of dealing with rejection from the outside world is to be motivated by what you are doing, as opposed to the attention you are getting for it. Which can be extra difficult, because getting attention (and thus being paid for it) is how you make a living from your art. Even so, it behoves you to relax, and it certainly won't do you any harm to work on your craft as opposed to your 'career'. Sheila looks at it like this: 'Whenever I get upset that another musician who I think is not talented is getting an opportunity I don't have, it reflects back to me my wish that the music world was more of a meritocracy. But who am I to judge who should get which opportunities? It's not for me to say. What I have to do is accept how the world *is*. I have to accept the things I can't control and focus on the things I can – like working on being good at my craft.' Or, as Henry Miller advised, 'We can stop thinking of what we have failed to do and do whatever lies within our power.'

David Munro, award-winning filmmaker, agrees. 'Cynicism is something to guard against, because it kills your love for what you are doing,' he says. 'When I was focused on not making it, I resented film. I couldn't even watch films. It became "poor me", and that is *death* when you're trying to attract people to fund your projects. If they smell that neediness, the deal is over. You have to talk to people like everyone wants what you're doing, whether they do or not. That takes a lot of practice.'

And a lot of self-discipline. The urge to spill one's guts wherever you happen to be standing at the time *must* be resisted. Yes, it's competitive. Yes, you have to witness people a lot less talented than you doing well. Yes, it's a crap shoot. Yes, some idiot will pronounce you too pretty to be a saxophone player. Or, you're just not getting the breaks that everyone else is getting. Or, you're too old. Or, too young. Or, too beautiful to be taken as a serious photojournalist. Or, too fat to be an actor. Or, too short. Or, your husband/wife is a famous author and you feel over-shadowed by them.

This is when you must get a grip. Novelist Mary Wesley was not too old. Joss Stone at sixteen was not too young. Roseanne Barr was not too fat. Christina Amanpour is not too beautiful. Sade is not too short. There is no such thing as 'too' anything. There is only how you feel about yourself. Ignore that destructive voice in your head; if you can't say anything nice about yourself, don't say anything at all, and try one – or all – of the tips at the end of this chapter to get your mood back to where you can be more positive and pleasant to be around, because being *un*pleasant is not going to get you anywhere. You know you're going to keep going ahead with it, so you might as well bite the bullet.

Being an artist is a little like having a terminal illness. You have to guard against any kind of negativity. When you're struggling for your very life, you don't focus on your eighty per cent chance of not surviving. You focus on the other twenty per cent. You stay away from naysayers and doubters and the people with stories about how Uncle George had the same thing and was gone in six weeks. You surround yourself with cheerleaders who also believe you can make it. You go out of your way to be around other survivors, who inspire you to realise you can do it too. You pray. The important thing is you stay positive by any means necessary and realise what my friend Mansur says to me all the time: 'The only person who can stop what's coming to you, is you.'

Even during my deepest depressions I have never really regretted having made the effort. Even just one year into being a singer, with not even a demo and hardly any gigs, I thought, 'If I get run over by a car right now, my last thought will be, "At least I tried. If there is such a thing as a next life, maybe I'll get to pick up where I left off."'

HOT TIP

Take care of yourself. Make sure you eat your vegetables. Really! It is easy when you are feeling down to let everything go by the board – especially if you live a freelance life where you don't have daily contact with people. Eat regularly and well. Make sure you have fresh vegetables and fruit. Make it a habit to get up at a regular time, shower and get dressed *before* you start working. It will give you a sense of being ready for the day. Make sure you are earning enough money to get by (in whatever way necessary if you are not making enough money as an artist yet) and not sink into debt. In other words, treat yourself as the ideal mother would treat you.

WHEN THE LIVING IS EASY

Everyone has talent. What is rare is the courage to follow that talent to the dark place where it leads.

Erica Jong

Depression can hit when you are on a roll. And when that happens it can be even more difficult to deal with because it doesn't make sense. At a very early point in my career, I found myself on the telephone to the Samaritans at five o' clock in the morning, sobbing uncontrollably about my life. I had just got my first manager, I had just won the unsolicited interest of a big record label, I had a wonderful supportive crowd that paid to come and hear me sing, an NPR radio programme had asked me to get in touch with them about appearing on their show. Things were going well. I should have been feeling wonderful. Understandably this made absolutely no sense to the young woman at the end of the Samaritan hotline and she hustled me off the phone, even though I'd told her I was feeling suicidal. Luckily my ex-boyfriend was at home to take the call I made to him straight after that one.

I don't blame her. She was probably inexperienced and was used to people calling up with 'real' problems. However, the point about depression is that it doesn't need to be linked to 'real' problems. Mental and physical health problems are the great equalisers in life. Millionaires are as prone to suffering as homeless people. 'Successful' people are as prone as unsuccessful. As Keith Jarrett wrote about having a great review, 'I looked at the review from the New York Times and said "Wait a minute, something's wrong. I'm supposed to feel good about this." Contrary to feeling good, I went into a deep depression.'

Sheila Cooper experienced something similar the first time she performed at the prestigious Maryanne's Jazz Room in Switzerland. 'I had a week at this great club. I had a kind of a patron, a generous woman who was helping me out. I was on the gig with Kenny Drew Junior and I found myself thinking, "How come these people are stupid enough to think I should be here?" My sensible self was saying, "Yeah! I belong here!" But my other self was thinking, "You're wrong. This is a mistake!"'

Perfectionism is what inspires us to keep growing as artists, but letting perfectionism take over is always counter-productive. You are there for the people in the gallery, not just for yourself. If you are giving them pleasure and *they're* loving it, that's perfect enough.

The gig actually went well, but what Sheila had to go through prior to each night's performance was hell. 'I'd feel angry and in a bad temper, just out of fear. Then afterwards I'd be excited. It's so primal I can't even explain it,' she says. 'You can say to yourself that you're good enough, but a part of you doesn't get it, so you just have to get up there and *do* it.'

I had a similar feeling the very first time I sang in a nightclub in London, when I sat in on a friend's gig and sang one song. It went really well. The band members all came over to me in the break and said how much they loved my voice. A woman in the crowd told the friend I was with that if I were a horse she'd bet on me. I felt absolutely elated all the way home. But then, just as I was putting the key into my front door, I was overwhelmed with a strong feeling of self-loathing. I felt actually physically dirty. I have no idea why. I just knew that it wasn't *allowed* for me to feel good about getting up and singing. Like Sheila says, the feeling is 'primal' it's so deep.

Depression can sometimes hit when you're not devoting enough time to the rest of your life and are focusing only on work. When TV show host Daphne Brogden was working on *The X Show* for FX Cable TV and at the same time doing a weekly show for TIVO, she crashed. 'I was thinking, "What's wrong with me? I've got two shows, I am earning six figures, I should feel great!" But I realised that the problem was that I was out of whack. I'd lost touch with my friends. I was all work and no balance. And then I had a secondary crash when my shows got cancelled. Then I *really* felt bad, because I didn't even have a social life to retreat to any more.'

Looking back, Daphne, now in a stronger place, realises what she did wrong. 'You have to create that space for your friends. You must schedule getting together with them just to play a board game or something. You mustn't let success take over.' Also a depressing factor at the top of the tree was the competition. 'It was constant,' says Daphne. 'All the jockeying for position – who'll get the comedy sketch or the interview – it's very hard to have real friends on a showbizzy set. And that is very alienating and depressing. Now I see I should have been more clinical about my work friends. Instead I got my feelings hurt.'

She also wishes she had spent more time with her non-work friends. There's an expression, 'It's lonely at the top.' People are jealous, or want to compete with you, or get something out of you. This is why it is imperative to know who your real friends are. They will keep you grounded. Taking a genuine interest in their lives will remind you that there are other things in life besides your career concerns, and sharing their successes and failures will keep you engaged in the world beyond Planet Ego.

USE IT AND LOSE IT

Art begins with resistance – at the point where resistance is overcome. No human masterpiece has ever been created without great labour.
André Gide

Yes, you can actually use your depression in your work and at the same time experience a cathartic release. 'The sacred space between pain and joy is the ultimate source for my musical expression and for my life's work,' says Quincy Jones. I have written some of my best humour pieces from the depths of despair, because I had a deadline for a magazine or newspaper and I simply had to meet it. I'd invariably feel cheered up afterwards. Miranda (see Chapter Five: Love Me or Leave Me) used her unhappy marriage as material for her novel. I sometimes use Nietzsche's saying, 'That which does not kill me makes me stronger,' as a kind of a mantra as I doggedly push past my bad feelings and carry on. Because, ultimately, of course, as long as you can hang in there, you *do* get stronger each time you manage to get through a period of depression.

HOT TIP
When a negative thought enters your head, practise just saying: 'Stop!' and focus your attention elsewhere.

Action seems to be the cure for most people. Former graphic designer turned painter Susannah Bettag sets herself deadlines – for example to have painted a certain number of pictures by a certain date. 'Then I know I have to go in and just paint, even if I'm not turning out anything I particularly like.' When all else fails she finds cleaning her studio helpful. 'I'll think, "It's time for a clean!" and it clears my mind,' she says. Another artist, painter and sculptor Becky Howland, finds that meditation helps her to focus and get her priorities straight, as well being a good way of easing into that experience of time alone that is necessary to being an artist. And she says she needs to work every day, 'Otherwise I get cranky.'

When she feels her inner critic take over she sets a cooking timer for fifteen minutes to an hour, during which time she works while suspending critical judgement. 'This is imperative for an artist,' she says. I find preparing for and doing gigs an absolute cure. It is soothing and focusing. And I have turned up to perform feeling so depressed that I didn't think I'd even be able to sing, let alone make witty repartee between songs. I now know never to worry about that because that is often when you sing your best. It's an incredible catharsis, and I miss it when I don't perform often enough.

You can use depression as a learning experience too, to improve your game. When that first label's interest in me fell through, it felt like the worst rejection. I flailed my arms and berated myself for my self-sabotaging response to their interest, focusing on all the things I did wrong, and the things I *should* have done instead. As novelist Karen Quinn, author of best seller *The Ivy Chronicles*, says, 'I think in any creative endeavour there are moments of great joy and moments when you feel like a complete fraud. I felt very much the same when I owned a small business. But when I was a lawyer or a corporate executive, the highs weren't as high and the lows weren't as low.'

At the end of the day, being an artist has to be about focusing on your art and your expression and improving and learning how best to do that, whatever your discipline. How long it takes, how much money you make along the way, whether someone else overtakes you 'unfairly', whether anyone else likes it or not, all these are irrelevant to your *journey*. 'I never let negative thoughts enter my thinking,' says singer Freddy Cole (brother of Nat King Cole). 'If you start thinking that way, it's going to end up that way. It doesn't mean you always win, but you will enjoy yourself.'

For Freddy, as with most artists, the practice of his art is its own reward. 'Being a musician you learn something new every day,' he says. 'There may not be any monetary gain. But when you sit down at your instrument you forget about the rent not being paid, the boyfriend, and your problems. All that consumes you is the music. And that's the greatest blessing you can ever have.'

How you can do it, too

When you're depressed it's very easy to think you don't have time to try any of the tips below. But please make an effort, because they do work, and if you're not even willing to try you must question your motives. Learn to entertain the possibilities.

1.   Be kind to yourself when you feel like those around you are not being kind. And don't berate yourself for having petty or unworthy thoughts and feelings. It is natural to feel upset at times with where you are in your career, or jealous of other people's success, or afraid of other people's envy, or despondent about finances or mistakes you have made, or being too casual, or too needy. Whatever you have done 'wrong', however you feel, the last thing you need to do is add to it by self-judging. Recognise your feelings for what they are – just feelings – and stop adding to your emotional discomfort by berating yourself.

2.   Accept what is. In *The Power of Now*, Eckhart Tolle reminds us of the Buddhist premise that emotional pain is 'always some form of non-acceptance, some form of unconscious resistance to what *is*.' This isn't to say that you should not try to change your circumstances. If not having money is depressing you, for example, the first thing to do is face and *accept* the truth that you don't have money. Then you can make a plan for getting some.

3.   Focus on the present moment. This ancient Buddhist exercise is a form of meditation. Take the next brief chore you have to do, washing dishes or making the bed, and focus all your attention on it. 'Recognising what we do with our minds, how unpresent we are, and how delicious whatever we're doing can be – these insights can make even the most mundane activities delightful and nourishing,' says Jean Smith

in *The Beginner's Guide To Zen Buddhism*. Try it. It works.

4.   Take up some form of meditation – even if it's only staring at a spot on the wall for ten seconds to start with, building up to twenty seconds, then ten minutes and finally twenty minutes. The point is to start. Daily meditation will help you with points 1 and 2, as well as calm your mind and body and make your life flow more easily. I don't always meditate every day but, when my life starts to fly out of control, regularly meditating again invariably gets me back on track. The book *Seven Masters, One Path* by John Selby offers guidance on the meditation techniques of seven great spiritual leaders.

5.   Acknowledge the source of your depression. It may be that you are about to move to the next level in your artistic development. The feeling of depression is just the normal feeling of dissatisfaction with where you are now. The best way through this is to focus on perfecting your craft. Amazingly, you will come through it – until the next time. In most cases, we come out of it, stronger than when we went into it. If you look back to some of your worst times, you invariably will have learned a valuable lesson.

6.   Get professional help. If you feel dangerously depressed, i.e. suicidal or self-destructive – do seek medical help. There is no shame in having the support of anti-depressant drugs for as long as you need them. I put off getting help for a long time because I was determined not to take medication. However, once I finally did my first thought was, 'Why didn't I do this years ago?' Of course the experience will vary from person to person. And being on medication won't *cure* your money or relationship problems, or even make you feel good about them. But in my case taking medication gave me a breather. I was still struggling with the artist-related issues described in this chapter, but I was more able to cope with my feelings, which allowed me the space to look at the issues

behind my depression and to deal with some of them. I still suffer the highs and lows, but with less intensity and I get over things more quickly. Anti-depressants give me a kind of inner strength that is otherwise lacking. I am not recommending them, but they work for me – despite my initial reluctance to take them.

7. Build up your self-esteem. Depression is often a symptom of low self-esteem. One way through this is to do things throughout the day that make you feel good about yourself. When I feel miserable, it is often because I am not taking good care of myself. Having a hot bath, giving myself a face pack, putting on lipstick – all these help me at times. So does exercise. You know what makes you feel better about yourself. Get a pen and paper and make a list of at least five things right now and look at that list the next time you feel bad and *do* something – even if it's only flossing your teeth twice a day for a week.

8. Get on with your work. I personally find work a great antidote to depression. I can go out and have a wonderful day and evening, come home at midnight and have my mood crash simply because I haven't achieved anything towards my dream at the end of the day. If you're feeling depressed day after day, try to do one small thing towards improving your career. Maybe pitch your work to a potential reviewer or gallery owner – never mind that you never hear a word back. Or sit down and work on your short story for even one hour. Sometimes the simple (and easy) act of doing my vocal exercises for twenty minutes will improve my mood – even if it felt like the very last thing I wanted to do before I did it.

9. Try to inject some regularity into your day. A daily exercise routine, a daily work routine, which holds you to regular hours, can give your life a sense of structure.

10. Call a friend. At particularly bad episodes I literally go through my address book from A–Z until I find someone at home. Always leave a message. Your friend may well want to help you. If it is too late to call a friend, call the Samaritans Hotline. There will always be someone somewhere who is available. It may be hard to remember this in the moment of feeling you are an unworthy blob that the world would be better off without, but I *promise* you, a friend would far rather be woken up by you in tears in the middle of the night, than be told that you threw yourself under a train, as sadly a brilliant friend of mine did a few years ago.

11. Limit your alcohol intake. Alcohol is a depressant. It may blot out the pain momentarily, but ultimately you will feel worse than if you didn't drink. The same goes for binge eating. It may stuff down your feelings momentarily, but the effect it will have on your self-esteem afterwards will not be worth it. When the urge to indulge in a binge of any kind overtakes you, distract yourself with a bath, a nap, a walk, a phone call to a friend. Many of today's most successful stars don't drink. There's a reason for that.

12. Put on a favourite piece of music. People have told me many times that my CD has helped them through a depression – maybe because I was processing my own depression at the time I recorded it and the songs I chose are either cathartic or ultimately optimistic. Do *not* listen to maudlin music, however. This will only make you feel worse – unless it's the *actual* blues. I have a marvellous mixed tape of the blues and to make me laugh I only have to hear Marlena Shaw singing about putting her head on the railroad track and getting up again because, 'Hang on, Marlena, you ain't paid for the hat!' or B.B. King sing the line, 'I gave you seven children, and now you want to give them back!' I also have in my video collection a couple of what I call 'PMS movies': *When Harry*

Met Sally and Emma Thompson's *Sense and Sensibility*. I've seen these movies countless times but watching them always cheers me up. Whatever movies you choose, the main thing is that they show triumph over adversity – like, say, *Billy Elliot*. Make a list of the most inspiring movies out there and watch them when things seem hopeless.

13. Join a support group: book clubs, writing groups, anywhere you are surrounded by like-minded peers.

14. Laughter really is the best medicine; watch a funny movie or read a funny book that always works for you. When I used to feel down, reading Nick Hornby's *High Fidelity* used to cheer me up completely. It's so simple you may not think of doing it.

15. Take yourself out of your life. Go and help out at a charity to remind yourself that you are a part of a bigger world and you have something to contribute.

16. Take a break. If you've been stuck in all day (or for days on end), writing/painting/composing/guzzling ice-cream/ 'angsting' in your PJs, *get out*! If you can honestly look yourself in the eye and say you have been overdoing it, take yourself to an afternoon movie or play. Or go on an inspirational 'artist date' as Julia Cameron calls them in her marvellous book *The Artist's Way*. That way you can kill two birds with one stone and have a rest at the same time as get inspired. I practically ran home from a wonderful Giacometti show at New York's MOMA in order to compose. Or just take yourself out for a coffee, like my writer friend Jane. 'Just the change of scenery does wonders for me,' she says.

Had there been no difficulties and no thorns in the way, then man would have been in his primitive state and no progress made in civilisation and mental culture.

Beck

Chapter Eight:
I'm Just a Jealous Guy:
Competition, Envy and the
Green-eyed Monster

A great band like that and they have to play with Ella. That bitch!
Billie Holiday

This chapter is about how to tame the green-eyed monster of professional jealousy; how to identify it in *you* if (or when) it rears its ugly head, and how to move beyond the jealousy that other people feel towards you that might hold you back if you let it. Because, if there is one truth in the arts, there is *always* going to be someone more successful than you to envy, and someone less successful than you to be envied by, so you'd better learn to handle it from both sides if you're going to survive with your sanity intact.

And if you are one of those rare saints who never feels jealous of other people, you may want to read this chapter anyway to gain some insight into those people who might be jealous of you. Or to arm yourself in advance of the possibility that – God forfend! – *you* suddenly find yourself turning into the evil green monster further down the road.

'My jealousy roars in the head, tightens the chest, massages my stomach lining with a cold fist as it searches out the best grip,' writes Julia Cameron in the (disappointingly small) section of *The Artist's Way* devoted to professional jealousy, which I had turned to one day in a desperate jealous frenzy, not knowing how to deal with it.

In days of yore, before I began singing professionally, I would have had no idea what she was talking about. I loved singers. I ran to check out all the new ones (I'd be the one shushing the talkers in the crowd). I joined all the mailing lists. I loved going to hear them sing. I didn't critique their intonation if they sang out of tune, or dismiss them as 'too technically perfect' if they sang *in* tune. And I certainly didn't sit in judgement at the start of a performance, with my arms and legs crossed, miming, 'Show me!' All things I have since witnessed other singers do. My guitarist and I used to make each other laugh by pointing out the people in the crowd who we could tell were singers there to check me out, just by their body language. To add insult to injury, they were invariably also talking throughout the entire performance (even the ballads) – especially if they had come with another singer.

I couldn't comprehend the pettiness of those around me who seemed to despise talented singers, merely because they were also good-looking, or young, or (worse!) both. I – saintly, wonderful I – was *thrilled* when people I vaguely knew became successful, because it gave me hope. It made me realise that success was within the realm of possibility. And when I went to the Manhattan School of Music to study vocal jazz, I was bewildered – and appalled – to discover that many of the singing faculty, far from being colleagues who admired and supported each other, viewed each other as rivals, sometimes with a fervour that seemed to border on hatred. I'm not talking about healthy competition (more on which later in this chapter), I'm talking about sheer, raw, unadulterated jealousy. And I could see it eating them alive.

I wonder now if they even realised what they were suffering

from. While doing the research for this chapter I found it very difficult to find people who would admit to having jealous feelings at all. The problem with jealousy is that it is *so* taboo that people often have trouble recognising it in themselves. I have a colleague who, if ever I get a flattering review, invariably writes me a sweet, congratulatory note, in which she *always* points out that the same reviewer gave her an even better review. I'm convinced she has no idea what she's doing – beyond making herself feel better about my good fortune.

But judge not, lest ye be judged. As I said in the previous chapter, at my worst, I couldn't bear to go and hear other singers perform live, and I certainly couldn't read good reviews – although I have yet to write and inform anyone I had a better one than they did. And I didn't even listen to the radio, for fear that it would upset me if I heard a colleague getting airplay. Then I'd hate myself for having such unworthy feelings – particularly if the object of my envy was a nice person. Sometimes I even *liked* them. Annoyingly, some very nice people are talented *and* successful. How much easier it is to resent an egomaniacal, dismissive, ungenerous talent who fancies themselves.

HOT TIP
If you feel jealous of other people, forgive yourself. Stay calm. Realise that it is perfectly normal to feel envious and/or jealous of other people's success when you yourself have been struggling unsuccessfully forever. When you have been trying to get your work into some gallery and someone you know gets in ahead of you, it would be weird if you *didn't* feel jealous. Stay calm. Use that feeling to inspire you to work harder. Understand that *your* time will probably come if you just keep going.

Over the years I have learned to identify, or at least suspect jealousy in myself – for example, whenever I feel a nebulous dislike for someone I do not even know (clue number one), who also happens to be doing better than I am (clue number two). When I feel like that it usually turns out to have been caused by the feeling that they have more than I do. Or, if I'm feeling particularly despondent, more than I'll *ever* have. But jealousy is hard to own up to, perhaps because it has been drummed into us since childhood that envy is one of the seven deadly sins.

Or maybe, because it is such a painful feeling, we think that by denying it even to ourselves we can make it go away. If only. Because, make no mistake, jealousy is a powerful emotion and, like love, to quote the song 'Fine and Mellow', it can make you do things '. . . that you know is wrong' – even murder, as postulated in the movie *Amadeus*, a fascinating study of composer Antonio Salieri's burning jealousy of Mozart.

IT ISN'T EASY BEING GREEN

No tree has branches so foolish as to fight amongst themselves.

Indian saying

Skater Tonya Harding got her hired henchmen to club the knees of rival skater Nancy Kerrigan before an important contest. And still she didn't prevail. Six weeks later Kerrigan won the Silver at the Winter Olympics, while Harding finished eighth, after missing all her jumps – blaming it on loose skates. Nearly six months after the attack, the U.S. Figure Skating Association stripped Tonya Harding of her 1994 national championship and banned her from the organisation for life.

At the time I would watch the news reports of the story with a sort of vicarious glee – my flatmate and I taking it in turns to champion one or other of the two women. But now that I have had a taste of it myself, I feel more compassionate and understanding, to the extent that when I first came across the quote from Billie Holiday that opens this chapter I laughed out loud, (a) from recognition and (b) at the absurdity of it – because I don't prefer Billie or Ella Fitzgerald over the other; I love them both, just as I love different songs for different reasons.

I have learned to (mostly) forgive myself for feeling these, what I call 'unworthy' feelings. But, bumbling along envy-free, I experienced it like a bolt from the blue when I first got stabbed in the heart by my jealousy of a fellow singer. I'd never really experienced it before – beyond a momentary pang or two – and it felt like hell.

This wasn't like my brother, who calls himself my 'Favourite Brother', catching me hugging my 'Other Favourite Brother' and half-jokingly separating us with his hands while whimpering: 'Mine!' That's kind of adorable, never mind that he is over forty. No, this was *Blue Meanie mean*. It kept me up at night. It haunted my dreams (invariably ones in which the other singer was vastly successful). It tortured me for weeks. And it all started when another singer once confided in me one night at a jam session that she liked something indefinable I did when I sang and that she was going to identify what it was and copy it. Even worse, when I'd said, 'Oh, please *don't*!' she'd said, 'Oh, don't be silly, we're all magpies! We all copy each other!'

Next thing I knew I was right back in high school. 'It is far worse to *have* to copy than to be copied from,' teachers and family friends used to intone. But the thought of this person getting all the credit for *my* idiosyncrasies and phrasings was terrifying. Naturally, I wouldn't have given a fig if she'd been a talentless buffoon. Unfortunately, she wasn't. And armed with my ideas, so I thought, she was all set to become an overnight jazz superstar. She didn't, by the way, which gives me some hindsight perspective on the whole thing now. But *then*, waking up in a cold sweat from nightmares in which she was successful, and I *wasn't*, I wrestled with this demon painfully.

Of course there is such a thing as intellectual property theft. When stocks and bonds trader-turned-guitarist John was at high school, he secretly referred to his best friend, also a guitarist, as 'the intellectual property thief' because he was constantly stealing his ideas. 'The worst of it was that he'd convince himself that they were his ideas,' says John. 'In the business world, people protect their ideas by getting colleagues to sign confidentiality agreements. But it's more difficult with music, which is all about sharing.'

I know an incredible singer – legendary among jazz vocal connoisseurs – who has been flagrantly copied way beyond 'paying homage' by a younger singer who has built an entire career from the other one's style. Granted these two singers have different, equally beautiful vocal tones, but the copying of the style, phrasing, even age-appropriate material, is undeniable. It enrages me just to witness it. I can't imagine what it must feel like to be the copied one.

There's very little you can do about it if someone is determined to copy your style. The only way to deal with it is to go out and do your thing as publicly as possible without allowing yourself to be affected by it – not by changing yourself in any way, and certainly not by holding back from anything less than the full expression of your authentic self. And remember that they can never have the same feeling as you, because they can never *be* you. Remember the Virginia Woolf quote: 'Every secret of a writer's soul, every experience of his life, every quality of his mind is written large in his works.' In which case, the more someone copies you, the less their work can be the authentic expression of themselves. And it's that which you are after, not how many records or books you sell.

It's a thorny subject. As journalist John Naughton pointed out, in an article in the *Observer* in 2003, there's a long tradition of artists taking inspiration from their peers, which, it could be argued, benefits society as a whole through the dissemination of ideas: 'As Picasso said – and Steve Jobs famously repeated when explaining how the Apple Mac came to bear such a striking resemblance to the Xerox Alto – "minor artists borrow; great artists steal."'

It is certainly true that society progresses by standing on the shoulders of our forebears. Giacometti was famously influenced in his early career by African art – the roots of which are clearly evident in his later works, which – by then – could only have been created by him. On the other hand, if you want to be the first to come out with an idea you'd better protect it from the rivals in your field, if you are going to get the credit (which, in many cases, will mean the profit).

HOT TIP
Look closely at how those that make you jealous achieved their success so you can emulate it – without stealing their artistry, of course. Is it their energy? Their innovation? Just basic persistence? Their contacts? Write a plan detailing how you can achieve what it is that you envy in them that you currently lack.

BEHIND THE GREEN DOOR

No dancer can watch Fred Astaire and not know that
we all should have been in another business.
Mikhail Baryshnikov

When I first felt so threatened by my so-called rival, I allowed it to close me off to sharing my work to the extent that when a relatively well-known singer called and asked if she could sing my lyrics to a Jobim song, I hesitated and had to be counselled by a wiser friend that this was surely the whole *point* of my writing songs and lyrics. 'Imagine Joni Mitchell not letting other people sing her songs,' he said, pointing out how silly I was being. Now I am thrilled when a singer asks if they may sing my compositions, and take these requests as the compliments they are. Art is about sharing your vision with the world, not jealously guarding it.

On the other hand, there is no reason I should allow people to record my compositions for free. A composer like any other artist is entitled to make money from their work. That's why permissions fees and copyright laws exist. But when you are talking about something as nebulous as a 'style', it is harder to protect. And lest you think this is something that only affects the obscure and struggling, it is said that the world's greatest tenor sax player, Charlie Parker, deliberately never recorded his best solos because he was so afraid of being copied.

But the most painful thing of all during this initial bout of jealousy, was how it made me feel about this new horrid me. This *stranger*. It's even harder if you like to think of yourself as all sweetness and light, which most people (including myself) do. On the other hand, when you are a creative artist you must be prepared to have the worst in you brought out into the open. And I have to confess that whenever my friend and musical mentor Mansur *dares* to talk admiringly about another singer, I say: 'But I'm your *favourite* singer!' And I am quite sure if he *hugged* one in front of me, I would be a total baby and cry: 'Mine!'

I know it's wrong. I know it is absurd. I know it is unnecessary. I don't understand it. Maybe it's just a primal memory response to growing up as the skinny, gawky brunette to my brother's adorable brown-eyed platinum blond. But I still feel it. So the first thing to realise is that jealousy happens – and to the best of artists.

I know I keep holding her up to illustrate my points – her fault for being such a prolific journal writer – but Virginia Woolf was horribly jealous of Katherine Mansfield, who was horribly jealous of . . . you've guessed it, Virginia Woolf. John Lennon is quoted as saying: 'I'm sick of reading things about Paul is the musician and George is the philosopher, and I wonder where I fit in. What was my contribution? I get hurt. I'm sick of it.' When novelist Muriel Spark won the writing competition that kick-started her career, one of the first things she did was give £50 of her prize money to a fellow struggling writer. Her rival never spoke to her again. As Bono says: '[Artists] are not the most secure people in the world.' But seen from our perspective as outsiders this pettiness seems completely unnecessary, even absurd.

And it can get *really* absurd. Author Alison Owings never feels jealous of good male writers, only female writers. Julia Cameron says she was never jealous of women novelists but did take 'an unhealthy interest in the fortunes and misfortunes of women playwrights.' A singer friend confided in me that she never feels jealous of good singers, only of bad singers doing well. I don't feel jealous of bad ones, only good ones – doing well or not.

And writer Kathryn Chetkovich, in *Best American Essays, 2004*, wrote a brilliantly, searingly honest account of the professional jealousy she felt towards *her own then-boyfriend*, Jonathan Franzen, during the course of their relationship when the publication of his novel, *The Corrections*, took him from struggling writer to critically acclaimed international best-selling author. In that essay she acknowledges the corrosive role envy played in their relationship. Not surprisingly, he is married to someone else now.

Good for Chetkovich for owning up to her demons. But what of handling other people's envy? When writer Marina dared to muscle in on her husband's turf ('He'd been asked by a friend to come up with ideas for some comedy sketches,' she says), he was furious. 'One day I thought of something on the bus on the way home and I ran into the house, terribly excited, shouting "Charles! Charles! I had an idea for a comedy sketch!" And he went bonkers, shouting at me that I hadn't been asked to come up with ideas, *he* had, and to butt out. He didn't even ask me what the idea *was*. Naturally, I've forgotten it now.' And the success of Alaa El Aswany's book created a great deal of envy among his peers. 'At one point the jealousy from other writers got so bad that I thought about moving to New Zealand,' he says. 'But to leave the Middle East would be death to an Arab writer so I stayed.'

It can be very difficult not hold yourself back in your career when confronted with the jealousy of other people, especially when you think it might lead to getting your knees clubbed – metaphorically or otherwise. As a child I was so afraid of hurting people's feelings by being better at something than they were, I even found myself walking agonisingly slowly behind old men in the street for fear that my youthful stride, if I overtook them, would make them feel old and bad about themselves.

And I was tortured by my classmates for being the class boffin, until, at twelve years old, I discovered being the class clown instead. It was great to be loved at last but, ultimately, my need to please (or rather not *dis*-please) other people made me smaller – and for years after I grew up I had an almost primal fear of other people's jealousy. Why else did I not even *try* to be a writer until I was thirty-one, despite having written stories and poems since I was about eight. And, as for singing . . . I'd wanted to be a singer for as long as I can remember, and yet I waited until I was forty-two to step onto the stage.

So how do you deal with being the object of someone else's jealousy? When Nicole Kidman was riding high, her best friend in Hollywood, fellow Aussie Naomi Watts, was a struggling actress for ten years, before being nominated for an Oscar for her part in *Mulholland Drive*. Although Watts doesn't come out and say she was jealous of her friend, Kidman demonstrated admirably how to deal with a friend's potential envy. 'Nic told me to just hang in there, because one thing can turn on a dime,' says Watts. 'I was inspired by her. The fact that we came from the same place gave me hope.'

HOT TIP
Count your blessings. Focus on how far you have come, as opposed to how far you still have to go, or on how much more someone else has.

KEEP TALKING HAPPY TALK

A really great talent finds its happiness in execution.
Goethe

There are definite ways through this torture. 'It may sound simplistic,' says singer Kendra Shank. 'But when jealousy rears its head, what often helps me is to count my blessings and practise gratitude, which is the *last* thing you feel like doing when you're jealous. I just start saying "thank you" out loud for anything and everything I can think of: Thank you that I am breathing. Thank you that I have a roof over my head. Thank you that the sun is shining. Thank you that I have food to eat. Thank you for my friends who love me. Thank you that I have all my limbs. Sometimes I even make it into a song.'

'I have to admit that when *The Ivy Chronicles* came out and other books by first-time novelists also came out and did better than mine, I was jealous,' says businesswoman, turned painter, turned novelist, Karen Quinn. 'I wanted to see my novel on the *New York Times* best seller list.' However, in the middle of discussing these feelings one day at her writing group, she suddenly realised how ungrateful she was being. 'I thought to myself, "Hey, I wrote a book and got it published. I sold the film rights. Catherine Zeta Jones is going to play a character based on me in the movies." I have nothing to complain about.' Karen tries very hard nowadays not to give in to feelings of jealousy. 'When they come up I try to deny them,' she says.

'Just train yourself not to do it,' says Veronica Henry. 'There's no point. Don't look at the book charts or other people's reviews. Don't mix with other writers and hear about their massive marketing budgets and their launch parties. Not if you can't handle it, anyway. What's the point? None of it is going to make you a better writer, and the ensuing anxiety will make you take your eyes off the ball. That way madness lies! Just because you're not a book club choice doesn't mean your work isn't as good. And maybe one day it will be your turn.'

Another way to counteract the feelings of professional jealousy is to remind yourself to focus on your own growth as an artist and a human being. 'I ask myself, "What do I want to accomplish?"' says Kendra. 'For *me*, rather than to prove anything. What song do I want to learn? What new recording project do I want to start planning? Dig into the work itself. Once my attention is back on my own creative process and making music (which is fun!), I stop looking over my shoulder at what other people are doing.'

Stop comparing. This is your own life path and what matters is what you discover and learn and accomplish for yourself. It has nothing to do with what other people around you are accomplishing. There are always going to be people who are better or worse off than you are, and realising that there are people who are actually jealous of *you* puts things into perspective. Your business is to compete with yourself; to practise and perfect your art and be *your* best, as opposed to *the* best. It's not a race. Think about all the different artists that you love equally. Does Kate Winslet's success preclude Emma Thompson's? Of course not.

During the worst period of jealousy I have ever experienced, this was brought home to me by jazz pianist Kenny Werner's wonderful book, the brilliant, witty and *soul*-saving *Effortless Mastery*. The first time I read it (laughing all the way through with recognition), it effected an overnight cure! It helped me to focus on not having to be the best in terms of technical skill or vocal tone, and instead concentrate on the purpose of being an artist at all – the need to communicate. As Martha Graham once said, 'The audience is your only judge and your only reality. I made up my mind that I was going to rely on the audience and not just on those I had invited and who wanted me to succeed. Some people did not.' Your true audience is never jealous. They want you to be your best – for them.

However, it's not always easy to remember these things in the moment. I have discovered that spiritual growth is a two steps forward, one step back, three steps forward, five steps back endeavour which requires constant vigilance, and – although re-reading *Effortless Mastery* usually brings me to my senses – I am still not immune to jealousy. 'To be immune means to exist apart from the rubs, shocks, suffering; to be beyond the range of doubts; to have enough to live on without courting flattery, success; not to mind other people being praised,' wrote Virginia Woolf – who clearly wasn't immune at all. But I have learned to accept that it is a part of the process and I forgive myself for it and to be grateful, even, that my jealousy is there to show me how much further I still have to go, both in my career and spiritually.

As Julia Cameron says, jealousy is a 'tough-love friend', reminding her that she must reach out for what she wants and realise that 'the truth, revealed by action in the direction of our dreams, is that there is room for all of us.' In spite of what we may feel while in the throes of jealousy, the reality is that most professions are meritocracies. 'Watching people I know finding their way in the art world, getting into good galleries or finding an agent, there would be times when I'd feel pangs of jealousy,' says artist Susannah Bettag. 'But when I look at my artist friends, I see that the cream really does rise to the top. In the end it is encouraging because it makes me feel I can make it, too. That if you work hard and have talent, you will succeed.'

How you can do it, too

When people are jealous of you:

1. Recognise your *own* feelings of jealousy. It sounds strange, but dealing with your own jealousy will make it easier to deal with other people's. I learned to spot my jealousy by observing and recognising in myself the behaviour of people who were jealous of me. Use their jealous behaviour to increase your self-understanding.
2. Don't let fear of other people's jealousy hold you back. Obviously, the best remedy for this is to stop needing other people's approval to such an extent that you are willing to sabotage your own dreams in order to get it.
3. But if you're not ready to take that step towards independence yet, take a baby step. You can trick yourself by hanging out with successful people who are less likely to feel threatened by your success. And *their* success will encourage you to pull yourself up to their level without fearing recrimination.

When you feel jealous of other people:

4. Work on raising your self-esteem. If you are confident and happy you are less likely to suffer from jealousy. There are literally hundreds of helpful websites that give advice. Just type the words 'self-esteem' into a search engine. And remember, whenever you are tempted to blob out in front of the TV or eat a pint of ice-cream, you are acting counter to your best interests. Think beyond the 'bad' activity to how you will feel about yourself afterwards. Bad, right? Conversely, if, instead, you use your jealousy to spur you to call a club owner about a gig, or to set a goal to have painted a number of paintings by a certain date, you will feel good about yourself afterwards.

5. Recall a time when someone was jealous of you. How did it feel? Do you feel that their jealousy was justified? Realise that the person you are jealous of is probably feeling at least as inadequate as you do, and that when it's your 'turn' to have some success, they will probably feel jealous of you.

6. A little bit of healthy competition is good for you. Use your jealousy to sharpen your game.

7. Don't bemoan how some people have all the luck and nothing good ever happens for you. If a rival is getting into the best magazines or galleries or night clubs or Broadway shows, look at what they are doing right and do it too.

8. Trust in the universe. There's a saying that goes something like: 'It's your job to plant the seeds. But it's God's job to make them grow.' I personally find that a very soothing idea. It reminds me that it's the journey not the destination that's important. Put your head down and just focus on and enjoy what you have, rather than check out someone else's plate to see if they have more on it than you do. Panicking,

trying to control and getting jealous about other people is not going to help the situation. If anything, it will only make matters worse. And it will certainly make you feel worse.

9.   Accept that some professions simply are more merito-cratic than others and redefine what do you mean by 'making it'. Is it making a living from your art, enough so that you can live from it without worrying about the rent, or is it that you want your name in Marquee lights?

10.   I often find it helpful, when faced with any challenge, to think about whether the issue would matter to me on my deathbed. It invariably would not.

11.   It may help to remember that each person's life has its ups and downs. Whoever it is you're jealous of may be in a time of great activity and accomplishment now, but they will also have their down time. Just as you will have both.

Benny and Björn, I suppose, already had an idea of which one was going to sing the lead. I mean, they knew perfectly well our ranges and which kind of voice they wanted on a specific song.
And sometimes, I envied the choice of Agnetha, I must admit.
Anni-Frid Lyngstad

Chapter Nine:
Blues for Junior:
Taking Care of the Children

Children might or might not be a blessing,
but to create them and then fail them is surely damnation.
US science fiction author Lois McMaster Bujold

This chapter is about how to simultaneously serve the needs of both career and children, so that neither needs to suffer. There's an old Chinese saying that if you save someone's life, you owe it to them to make sure the rest of their life is happy. If you *give* someone life, that responsibility must be even greater. We've all heard the biblical commandment, honour thy father and thy mother, but if more people honoured their *children* it'd be a hell of a lot easier to do that. As it is, some parents should be strangled at birth, but our little baby hands are too small to fit around their big grown-up necks. Naturally, *you* aren't that sort of parent, or you'd have skipped over this chapter and gone straight to the one on success. Still, it bears pointing out, I think, that children don't ask to be born, we bring them here. We therefore owe it to our kids to make their lives as joyful as possible. And the best way to do that is to devote our *time and loving attention* to them.

The major problem to overcome is that, if we are seriously involved in the creative arts (creative projects are invariably referred to as an artist's 'baby'), it can be hard, depending on your discipline, to negotiate giving your children as much time and attention as you'd like to – and vice versa. As artists of all disciplines realise, there is no real 'time off' when you are a freelancer. Work is on your mind at all times (rather like children are) whether you are actively doing it or not. But some professions are less demanding than others. For example, I found it relatively easy to go back to school and then become a writer, in terms of the time it left over for my son. Most of the time I could fit my studying or writing around his hours and needs, and work when he was asleep in bed. And everyone has heard about JK Rowling, an impoverished single mother, sitting in a café to save money on the heating, scribbling the story of *Harry Potter*.

But music is absolutely my baby and, just like a baby, it doesn't fit in with me, I fit in with it. I know some people can probably do both, but if I had been a musician when my son was a child, I don't think I would have been able to do justice to either – at least not as a single parent. Explaining to my son that I was on a deadline and that I wouldn't be able to play with him all afternoon was one thing. At least he'd still be in the general orbit of 'Planet Mum' – which, as I spend more and more time with my friends' young children lately, I realise is of the utmost importance. But being available to travel to St Louis for two days followed by two days in California and possibly Seattle a week later, would have been a lot harder to negotiate – especially once his schooling became involved. Yet, if I'm not available for gigs, I don't earn money.

Renee Knight, who was a BBC documentaries director for twelve years, eventually gave up her very successful directing career within a few years of having children. 'There was no way I could be available to do something like all-night editing once I had two kids,' she says. When my son was nineteen, a photographer I knew suggested we do a story on a prison in Mexico where the criminals ran free. I told her that, as a parent, I wasn't in a position to risk my life. But even fashion photography, which often involves being sent off to exotic destinations for a week at a time, would probably be hard with young children. Painting, possibly less so.

However, there are ways to negotiate giving your best to both career/creative expression *and* children or, as in Renee's case (she now writes TV scripts), make a complete career change. It may be that having kids even inspires you to greater things.

I GOT YOU BABE

Frankly as fun and entertaining as the entertainment business is,
it pales in comparison to raising kids – for me anyway.
The glamorous parts of business are indeed glamorous,
but they're fleeting and fickle.
Julia Louis-Dreyfus

I know several women, and one or two men, who have actively picked their careers over having children at all. But, in my experience, having a child is one of the most inspiring things you can do for your art – even if you have to wait until they are an adult to pursue it. Avant-garde musician Kyoko Kitamura found that the birth of her son, which occurred at around the same time as her mother went through a life-threatening illness, 'deepened' her music.

'I may be rusty in technique and ear training and all the stuff they teach you in school,' she says. 'But I have received something else that can only be gained through experience. Being consumed by love for this tiny human being who is so dependent on you in such a complete way, it seeps into every aspect of my life. How can this *not* affect my music!' The downside is that she now has less time for it. 'If I'm lucky I have an hour a day to practise, so the time I devote to it is small. On the other hand, I have learned to be more *present* when I practise.'

'I had a radiant pregnancy, filled with creative energy, as if the miraculous physical impetus to create and grow the baby inside galvanised my artistic life,' says singer and saxophonist Sheila Cooper, whose best gigs have happened since her daughter Calli was born. 'It's been a life-changing experience to be a mother. I had some wonderful playing experiences during that time.' But enduring the first three weeks of Calli's life with her in neonatal care in respiratory distress was what really put things into perspective. 'Standing by her bed, wringing my hands in the agony of powerlessness, looking into the abyss of, "What if she dies? What if she dies? My life will simply be over!" caused an unstoppable reordering of my priorities. It really makes a "career" small potatoes.'

The detachment which that feeling afforded Sheila was very liberating artistically. 'Except now, of course, there's no time, and often no physical energy, to do things like practise, write arrangements, do business. So you have to work smart – you have to make more money in less time,' she says. 'Necessity is the mother of invention, though, and necessity has galvanised me into manifesting some good gigs for myself.' It helps that Sheila's husband, saxophonist Andy Middleton, is also a musician and very much a hands-on father, which enables them both to spend more time with Calli than kids with two nine-to-five parents. Calli has toured Europe with her parents seven times in her five-year-old life, including a month-long tour when she was only four months old, and Andy came along solely to do the childcare. 'We were together the whole time, except when I was on stage. Although I must admit that is something only a new mother would be naïve enough to do. I was exhausted.'

It's not easy. Andy and Sheila don't have as much control over their schedules as they would like. 'And sometimes Calli has to deal with babysitters several nights in a row, and that starts to get to her,' says Sheila. 'There's some kind of critical mass she hits, like the other night, where she literally splayed her little five-year-old body across the doorway as I was trying to leave and cried, "You can't go to your gig!" A rare event, but heartbreaking.'

Sheila has also had some minor health problems, largely brought on by exhaustion from overworking and 'taking care of all that being a freelance musician entails at the same time as being as good a mother as I can be. But every morning when I wake up, my first thought is how much I love my child and how happy I am that I'm her mother. She brings so much joy to my life, and I've definitely seen that joy come into my music.'

Some people find that having children helps them to crystallise their creative calling. When 36-year-old Alex had Emma she was a multimedia producer for a major film production company. 'It was very hard work,' says Alex, 'I was in charge of about fifteen designers and writers and it was pretty stressful.' When Emma was born Alex took six months off to stay home with the baby. 'I enjoyed it because after working full time for ten years I needed a break from it.' Then, when her company offered her voluntary redundancy she jumped at the chance to escape.

'I thought I could freelance here and there to keep my hand in until Emma was old enough to go into daycare,' she says. 'My husband was working so we didn't really need the money urgently.' In reality Alex found it very hard to get work as a freelancer ('I admit I didn't try very hard') and before she knew it, she'd lost most of her contacts. 'By the time Emma was three, I wasn't in a position to get back into the business – even if I'd wanted to. It's very fast-changing technologically, and I was no longer up to speed,' she says. 'I knew I didn't want to go back, but I wasn't really sure what I did want to do.'

In the meantime, she felt dissatisfied with 'just' being a mother, and felt isolated at home, because all her other friends were working. 'A child isn't stimulating intellectually, and while I love Emma very much, I needed another outlet for my creativity. I started writing during the day while Emma was having her nap. Being around Emma gave me an idea to write a young children's comic book about a child superhero with magical powers, and I just decided that I would make time for it. I would get up an hour earlier and devote that hour before Emma woke up to working on it, and another hour while I dropped her off to a neighbourhood babysitter.' She is still working on the comic book. 'I'm very happy to be doing my two hours a day. It makes me feel productive and as if I haven't given up on life outside of being a wife and mum.'

Many women feel a loss of identity when they give up work to look after the children. In her memoir of post-partum depression, *Down Came the Rain*, Brooke Shields writes, 'Although being a mother is not the only thing I am, it further defines me. I realise I can be a mother and have a career. I think I feared losing myself when I have a child . . . now I see I've gained even more of who I am.'

Renee Knight felt very much the same when she gave up directing documentaries to stay home with the children. 'I would dread going to parties, because when people asked you what you were doing and you'd say, nothing at the moment, because I'm at home with the kids, you'd see their eyes glaze over,' she says. 'I don't have an economic need to work, but I do need it emotionally.' She had an idea for a television screenplay and decided to work on it, starting out slowly working for two hours a day, and gradually upping the time she gave herself, once both children were in school. 'It's surprising, especially if you're used to obsessively working around the clock, but even squeezing in a few hours a day can yield concrete results – even success. It was a matter of doing that or going mad. I felt I had no choice,' says Renee, whose children were eight and five. It took about a year to finish her first screenplay, but then, via contacts, she sent it to an agent who loved it and took her on. She has subsequently been commissioned by a broadcaster to write a second television screenplay.

And it isn't only women who are faced with having to choose. When children's book author Mal Peet met the mother of his two eldest children he had already published a literary criticism book on poetry, illustrated one or two other books and published a few cartoon strips. However, two children (thirteen months apart) later, it became impossible for both him and their mother (then a part-time psychologist) to pursue poorly paid careers, and he was chosen to be the main breadwinner as well as part-time stay-at-home parent. 'I had to work part time for cash as a plumber and builder. Looking after the kids was fun but I hated the building work,' he says. 'But although you can live hand to mouth, it's just not possible to live hand to *three* mouths, so I had no choice.'

Or so he thought. In fact, his then partner's jealousy of his writing was more of a barrier to his creativity than children or work. 'At one point I was trying to collaborate with a friend on a comic play and she could hear us laughing upstairs while she was downstairs with the kids. When I would come down to make a cup of tea or something, she'd say things like, "You haven't seen the kids for two hours" or "Isn't Daddy neglectful!" In the end, I did nothing creative for six years in that relationship.' Then, two years after that relationship dissolved, Mal met his wife, Elspeth Graham. 'I was still plumbing, and my life after work consisted of coming home every evening, eating a bowl of brown rice and getting into the bath with a Dickens novel and four cans of Tennants Super. I was very depressed,' he says.

And now he had three children to worry about, including Elspeth's 18-month-old son. But Elspeth, who felt that he was wasting his talent, encouraged him to get back into writing again while she shared the financial burden by teaching. 'The first thing we did was collaborate on a book idea which won the interest of an editor at Walker Books, who liked us enough to point out what we were doing wrong, and three years later, we were actually scraping a living from writing,' says Mal, who has since collaborated with Elspeth on over a hundred children's picture books. 'It was hard, because if the kids were over on the weekend of a deadline and Elspeth drove them home instead of me I wouldn't hear the end of it from their mother, but I persevered in the belief that it would pay off in the end.'

Like so many of the artists I have interviewed (let alone me), Mal thought that he would achieve success sooner. 'When we got a four-book contract we were convinced that vast wealth was just around the corner and I'd be a better breadwinner, but of course it took longer,' he says. But it was worth it. Mal recently won the Branford Boase Award for best first novel, as well as the Nestlé Book Award for his book *Keeper;* his just-published novel *Tamar* is receiving wide acclaim and he has just delivered his third novel. Meeting Elspeth was the turning point. She not only encouraged him and believed in him, she facilitated his writing. 'Most of all, if you have kids, what you really need your partner to give you is time,' says Mal.

Time was very much the issue for Lucy Berrington, who had always wanted to be a fiction writer, but stopped writing after college and became a freelance journalist, which she gave up when her first child was born. 'But when my eldest was two, I started writing again. I needed an identity beyond being a mum, and I had got out of journalism and I thought well, I've got to write *something,*' she says. 'I once read an interview with a male pop star who suggested that the reason that men were more creative than women was because women have kids and don't need the outlet. And I realised that he just doesn't get it about finding time. When does a mum find three straight hours in a day?' Indeed, when we look back into the annals of female art history, we can see that of all the great talented artists very few were mothers. All the Brontë sisters, Frida Kahlo, Virginia Woolf: none had children. It is only in the last century that women artists have come into their own, in terms of visibility.

So Lucy worked in tiny snatches when her son was napping or in bed. 'The reason I didn't write a novel was because I didn't feel I had the time, so I did short stories,' she says. 'It would have been hard to do something outside my experience then because I didn't have the energy. And the things intruding on your time are very important – baby gym, lunch, errands – so it's hard work. On the other hand, mothers have to learn to manage all the different, simultaneous demands of being a parent and I have brought some of those skills to writing. I can literally do ten minutes at a time, which is like bringing up kids – a bit here and a bit there.'

SOMETHING'S GOT TO GIVE

If there is anything we wish to change in the child,
we should first examine it and see whether it is not something
that could better be changed in ourselves.

Carl Jung

The time for your creative pursuit has to come out of *something*. Just make sure it doesn't take away from your kids. It is impossible to do everything, so you have to prioritise. When my son was fifteen I had a job on a magazine which necessitated my being there twelve hours a day plus weekends. Because I was building my career at that time, I just didn't feel that I could tell my editor that I was neglecting my home life. So I soldiered on. However, I felt horribly guilty about the fact that I wasn't spending any real quality time with my son. When, that year, he narrowly failed all his GCSEs, I felt entirely responsible.

The following year, I made sure that I was at home every evening to be a nurturing presence, to make sure he ate properly, and to ask him how his day had been. It really didn't require much more than that, but my presence made all the difference. He got straight As in the retakes. And as far as my career was concerned, I only took a temporary step backwards. It took me a while to get my mojo back when I went back to working full time, but being at home for those crucial couple of months was absolutely worth it and, ultimately, it didn't interfere with the progression of my journalism career. But if I hadn't been available to my son, it would certainly have impacted his future.

> **HOT TIP**
> Don't expect that kids when they are little will be supportive of you spending large chunks of time away from them.

June Daventry, a painter, had wanted to be an artist all her life. She won a scholarship to art college during the Second World War when she was evacuated to the country, but the family she was staying with hid it from her because they wanted her to go to work, winding cotton reels, so she could bring in money. Then one day while she was waiting for the train to take her to work she decided on a whim to take a train in the other direction to Gravesend, where she enrolled at the art school and did a degree. However, it took her all her life to become a painter because she had three children to support after her husband died. 'I took a degree in art history and taught,' she says. Only now is she truly a painter. 'Whatever age you are when you do it, the only way to be an artist is to step into the void,' she says. Something that back then would have been almost impossible to do with children.

Nowadays, women aren't expected to choose between career and kids in quite the same way. But juggling motherhood and artistic pursuit still requires some serious prioritising. 'Be willing to make some big sacrifices,' Lucy advises. 'You have to be disciplined. It might mean you don't see your friends as much as you want to. Or you might have to choose "Will I cook, or will I write and give the kids a microwave dinner?" I still think I can squeeze it all in, but I can't. If you're looking after a house and kids you literally have to let big things go, like cleaning the house.' Because, while it's true that your artistic pursuit might feel like 'your baby', the truth is, it's a baby that, unlike your real child, can be put aside for a month or two, or even longer, without it ending up in some Thai prison for drug smuggling a few years down the road.

And you never know when opportunity might come to you through your children. Carol Hall, who wrote the score for *The Best Little Whorehouse in Texas*, got a well-paid job writing advertising jingles by attending a PTA meeting at her school, where she met an advertising executive who'd heard that her song 'Jenny Rebecca' had been recorded by Streisand. 'I was being a good mum in going to the PTA meeting, because you say to yourself all the time, "I really ought to go to this party and network." You never say, "I really need to go to the PTA meeting." And it turned out to be the most important thing that happened to me back then. It was the first year I ever made money with a comma in it. I felt like a millionaire.' Karen Quinn, corporate lawyer turned author of best seller *The Ivy Chronicles*, was introduced her to her literary agent by her nanny.

PLAY TOGETHER,
STAY TOGETHER

My mother said to me, 'If you are a soldier, you will become a
general. If you are a monk, you will become the Pope.'
Instead, I was a painter, and became Picasso.

Pablo Picasso

Another thing you can do to give yourself more time for your
creativity and spend time with the children is to involve them
with your art and encourage them to find a creative expression
of their own. This will also help you to avoid a situation in which
your child is in direct competition with your vocation. If your
daughter hates the sight of your paintbrush, or has decided that
your word processor is the enemy, it will be torture. Jessica
Papin, a literary agent, grew up the youngest of five children of
artist and illustrator Joseph Papin. She has very clear memories
of her father drawing at the kitchen table, where he worked
despite the relative chaos of sketching in a room that was the
nerve centre of a noisy, kid-filled house.

'He was an on-scene artist, so he was good at shutting out
distractions, yet we never felt like we were shut out,' says
Jessica. He encouraged all of his children to draw, and when one
of Jessica's sisters decided that she was more interested in
theatre he was equally pleased. As a reportorial artist, his
assignments included covering the trials in New York federal
courts: 'When the cases were appropriate back then – when
neither a mobster nor murderer was on trial – my dad would
bring me along: armed with my own sketchpad. I felt terribly
important, and fiercely proud of my father.'

Karen Quinn took her thirteen-year-old daughter Schuyler
from New York to London for the release of *The Ivy Chronicles*.

'It was a good experience for her to see the book in all the store windows, the posters in the Tube stations, to be part of the party Simon & Schuster gave me. I want her to see her mother succeed so that she knows she can succeed at anything she puts her mind to. I never pursued careers in areas of my passions because my parents told me I wouldn't be able to make a living. I want Schuyler to go after her dreams and know she can succeed just like I have.'

If you can associate your work with fun in the minds of your children, you will, like Karen, inspire and engage them, and bring them squarely into your corner with you. Mystery writer Janet Evanovich has gone even further and got her entire family involved in the marketing of her Stephanie Plum series of books. Evanovich Inc is the family business, literally. And when her children were small, she says that they always understood why they never went on holidays like other families. '"You take your time and write!" they'd say,' she remembered, in a recent interview.

Your child doesn't have to follow entirely in your footsteps as long as they have some creative outlet to help them appreciate – let alone benefit from – the act of expressing oneself. It will give your child a greater understanding of you, which will bring you closer and give you something more to talk about, as well as be something you share in common. It goes without saying, of course, that you do not force your child into any particular form of creative expression – especially your own. If they hate it, it will increase any feelings your child may have about competing with your art.

And don't be a stage mum. Remember, you're reading this book for the sake of your own creativity, not to find out how to do hot-housing – a popular 80s (when else?) fashion for teaching your kids from the womb onwards to make them into geniuses. Besides which, everyone needs to have something of their own. If you are channelling your dreams through your children, you are not giving them a chance to have theirs. As Sufi poet Kahlil Gibran said: 'You are the bows from which your children as living arrows are sent forth.' In other words, children must be set free to choose their own destinies.

It is important when encouraging your children's creative expression not to tie it to having to be a vocation. When my friend James Bull told his parents he wanted to be a poet when he grew up, his father said, dismissively, 'What are you going to do, open a poetry shop?' Consequently James never got his writing off the ground. He is now an investment banker. But if you can't dream when you're a child, when can you dream? Don't crush your child's dream; learn from your child. As Yehudi Menuhin said, 'What guides us is children's response, their joy in learning to dance, to sing, to live together. It should be a guide to the whole world.' But it doesn't have to be a job. There are millions of happy accountants in this world who paint on the side. They don't all have to be Paul Gauguin and run off to Tahiti to do it full time.

HOT TIP
Encourage your children to have a creative outlet: and teach them to appreciate all the arts, not only the one that is your speciality: that way they can pick and choose the one that's best for them.

MOTHER'S LITTLE HELPERS

While we try to teach our children all about life,
our children teach us what life is all about.
Angela Schwindt

Being a parent is so all-consuming that you do need to call in reinforcements from time to time if you are trying to pursue your creativity. 'It is very difficult to work at any job and have children at the same time,' says Karen Quinn. 'I do the best I can, but the fact that I'm starting a brand-new career makes this twice as hard. Luckily my schedule is totally flexible so I can go to my son's Little League games and make my daughter's ballet performances.' Karen also has a babysitter who has been with the family since her daughter was born, thirteen years ago. 'She is like a third parent in this family. I don't think I could work this hard without her support.'

If you cannot afford full-time childcare, you might have to be a little inventive. When Elizabeth Kaiden, a New York City writer, decided to go back to work after the birth of her son, she realised that the cost of daycare would be almost as much as she was earning. She tried working from home for a while, but found she missed the community of working in an office. So she founded a nonprofit organisation called Two Rooms that provides office space and childcare in adjoining rooms (in keeping with the principles of 'Planet Mum') on a flexible basis for creatives and their young children. According to its mission statement, 'It presents a new solution for the nontraditional worker by providing resources for freelance and/or home-based workers who don't have the need or can't afford the expense of full-time childcare.' It also provides a much appreciated community for people in isolated professions, let alone isolated at home with the kids too. An idea to copy, perhaps.

I can't believe I've got this far into this chapter and not mentioned your partner. Children invariably have two parents, and they should both be taking responsibility for their nurturing and care. If your partner is the breadwinner, you may feel guilty taking time from running the home to pursue your own work.

However, just because one of you is earning more money than the other doesn't mean you aren't working equally hard during the day. Contrary to some working partners' beliefs, running a home is not all coffee mornings, spa outings and watching daytime soaps. I remember being challenged one day by my husband, who came home from work and was appalled by the mess – especially since I was normally a neat-freak. 'What the hell have you been doing all day?' he said. 'Writing!' I said, defiantly. 'What? You think Simone de Beauvoir did house-work?' I'd just read *The Second Sex*, and was feeling put upon that I was not only doing all the housework, but that he didn't realise how much work it was.

Being a full-time parent is incredibly demanding, emotionally *and* physically. And it is a much easier task when shared by two people. Talk to your partner and come to some agreement about what it is reasonable to expect of one another. Clearly, when your partner comes home absolutely exhausted after a nightmare twelve-hour day you don't thrust a screaming, teething baby into his or her arms, as you retreat to your studio. However, it is not unreasonable in the evenings, after a fair wind-down period, to expect your partner to help with the dishes after dinner, to take it in turns to read the bedtime story, to chat to the children and you about your day – *because you have been at work all day too.*

When Jenny wanted to work on her ceramics, she had a very hard time getting her husband Bill to realise that she hadn't had time to devote to it during the day while he was at work. Of course, she'd been running around picking up after the children. But even more, she'd been picking up after him, because he felt entitled to leave a mess since he was earning the money and believed that she should be earning her keep. 'I remember asking him once to take the kids to the park for a couple of hours on a Saturday and it caused a huge row,' Jenny recalls. Bill, it turned out, was completely non-negotiable on giving Jenny the time off she needed, as well as on other issues, and they ended up divorcing. 'And then I found I had all the time I needed,' she says. 'In the first place it halved my household duties not having to pick up after him all the time, and on top of that he took the children every other weekend, so now I have entire weekends to devote to my passion.'

Of course, I'm not suggesting that we all get divorced in order to get free childcare. In a decent relationship you should be able to reach some understanding with your spouse. Aspiring writer Susan's husband made sure that her unpaid writing was honoured as much as his paid work. Leslie Ware, a professor of political science, and her husband, a photographer, decided that they would make time for *both* of their unpaid creative pursuits, Leslie as a painter and John as a musician. They alternate giving each other two-hour 'time grants' in which they can spend a guiltless Sunday afternoon on their projects. In addition, their children, who are now ten and twelve, are expected to pitch in with household chores. Leslie says, 'I was doing load after load of laundry, and I realised that while it was awfully time con-suming, it was also quite easy. The kids were perfectly capable of loading and operating the machine, and folding and putting away their own clothes. Thereafter, laundry time became my time.'

In fact, it is a great idea for your children to contribute to the housekeeping when they are old enough. When my son was thirteen, I decided that certain chores in the house could be done by him, including loading the dishwasher and vacuuming the staircase. Of course he grew to hate these tasks, but I pointed out to him that there was no earthly reason why I should have to clean up after everybody, and he understood, and bit the bullet – just like I did, when I did housework. Don't break down and take over because they're not very good at it.

They will only get good with practice. You must not be afraid to stand up for yourself and your creativity. Your child will not be scarred as long as you keep your expectations within reason. Obviously, don't be like Milton, who virtually enslaved his daughter, making the poor thing transcribe the whole of *Paradise Regained*. It's all about balance. I'm merely suggesting that your ambition to be a singer is *as* important as your husband's work and your son's passion for cricket, and that honouring all of these should be a shared, family responsibility. Your children would rather you worked on your painting than make them feel responsible for you not doing it before.

> **HOT TIP**
> Don't feel you have to do everything. You'll just exhaust yourself and be less available for your child and your art. Give yourself a break.

A ROOM OF ONE'S OWN

An unused life is an early death.

Goethe

Taking time off to be alone is a vital part of being an artist. Don't feel guilty. You are not an evil parent just because you need time away from your children. It's probably more healthy than being a clingy parent. If they don't understand, then sit them down and explain it to them. 'You can put your song on the CD player and prepare to be totally engrossed in the performance when your wife, girlfriend, brother, sister, even your mother asks you if you remembered to take out the garbage,' says lyricist Bruce Heckman. 'Your creation rarely means anywhere near as much to any other person as it does to you. When your loved ones wonder very out loud where you have been or why the piece you are working on means they can't spend time with you, stay cool. Tell them that it is not personal, that you hear the voices of the demons of Art telling you to be available to your muse totally and now. They will not understand but, if you are lucky, they will walk away shaking their heads muttering about getting the doctor to increase your anti-psychotic medications. The important part is "walk away".'

Lucy uses her writing, she says, as a break from her two boys. 'Parenting is so cluttered. There's so much going on all the time,' she says. 'When I'm writing away from the kids it's the ultimate thing to be doing for myself. It gives me space emotionally.' Karen Quinn says, 'It's so hard to fit it all in. But I always try to put the children first, although I have to admit that I've missed some of their important moments because of professional commitments. Who are these working women who say they never miss their children's events? They can't possibly be telling the truth. If you choose to work and have kids, you will miss out on some things. If you choose to stay home full time with kids, you will also miss out. There's no perfect way to live one's life.'

Mother of three Veronica Henry says: 'Just accept that this is an endurance test, and that you are the bottom of the pile. Your children have to come first, I'm afraid, and that's the end of it. Don't worry about matching table linen, try not to drink too much alcohol during the week and remember: one day in the not so very distant future you will have all the time in the world without them.'

How you can do it, too

1.   Always involve your children in any decisions you make around your career that will mean reducing the time you

spend with them. You may not be able to stay home, but you can make them feel that they are heard. For example, don't call home and say, 'I'll be two hours late.' Call and explain why you are delayed and ask them how they feel about it. Then listen and *respond* to what they tell you.

2. Engage your child's interest in your creative activities. Take kids on outings having to do with your career: to see the ballet, or hear jazz, or go to an art museum, or a play. You may be surprised at how sophisticated they are. When my son was eleven, I took him to see guitarist Stanley Jordan and McCoy Tyner in a double bill at the Royal Festival Hall. I fully expected him to prefer the more accessible Jordan. But he came away a big fan of the more musically challenging Tyner.

3. Enlist help. See what your kids need, and then find someone who can pick up the slack while you get on with your work – whether it's your partner or other family member, a nanny, a friend with whom you take it in turns to share childcare, or the occasional babysitter – funds allowing.

4. Carve out time each day for a particular ritual – something the kids can count on. Everyone can manage a five-minute story time. It will make them feel safe that yours is the last voice they hear before falling asleep.

5. Teach kids to respect mummy or daddy's quiet time. Create projects for the children that they can work on as you are working. Kids need quiet time, too. Everybody needs to regenerate.

6. Allot particular times to getting on with your creative work and make those times sacred.

7. Don't be afraid to take time out from your artistic pursuit to spend with your child. You might need to put your dreams on hold for a month or so at a time but you will catch up.

8.   Accept that there is a trade-off. No parent is perfect. Men and women with regular nine to five jobs obsess about being not good enough parents just as much as artists and others in creative fields.

On the one hand, people think they own kids;
they feel that they have the right to tell the kids what to do.
On the other hand, people envy kids.
We'd like to be kids our whole lives. Kids get to do what they do.
They live on their instincts.
David Duchovny

Chapter Ten:
Up, Up and Away: Success at Last

> You can be up to your boobies in white satin,
> with gardenias in your hair and no sugar cane for miles,
> but you can still be working on a plantation.
> *Billie Holiday*

When I started thinking about writing this chapter, it occurred to me that there are many more ways of defining success than the Oxford Dictionary definition of: 1. The accomplishment of an aim or purpose; 2. The attainment of fame, wealth, or social status. In fact, success is so relative, that one person's success could even be another one's failure. Or what you once considered the epitome of success may feel like nothing once you've achieved it, in which case you'll *never* achieve success – rather like the proverbial donkey chasing after the carrot. Sir Winston Churchill defined success as 'the ability to go from one failure to another with no loss of enthusiasm.' But, for the purposes of this chapter, we will assume that it *is* the attainment of fame, wealth, or social status, as opposed to simply being happy with your life (because they are by no means always synonymous). This chapter is about how to deal with some of the issues that might come up for you once you achieve this longed-for state.

The first thing is that, contrary to your expectations, success can be hard. I know, I know, pity actresses Drew Barrymore and Carrie Fisher – talented, rich, well-connected, beautiful. It must be a *nightmare*, poor things. But seriously, both Drew Barrymore and Carrie Fisher (the two of them also born into Hollywood royalty) did have a hard time handling success. Barrymore struggled with addiction throughout her so-called childhood, having her first drink at nine, first taste of marijuana at ten and first line of coke at ten. She went into drug rehabilitation at the age of only thirteen. Carrie Fisher's *New York Times* best-selling *Postcards From The Edge*, which won the Los Angeles PEN Award for best first novel, tells the story of a young star, whose story begins with having her stomach pumped, undergoing drug rehabilitation – all the result of early fame, and dealing with having a famous mother, rather like Fisher herself. And the list of 'success casualties' is long. So, judging by the examples of all those who have lived fast and – if they were unlucky – died young, it would seem that fame, wealth and social status, at least the instant kind, can cause a lot of those who achieve it to implode, often torpedoing their careers in the process. Just think of River Phoenix, who once said: 'Achieving success gets complicated. You find yourself hanging around with a different crowd. I probably would have shied away from it, but after a while you can't help but get sucked in . . . all those parties and premieres and limos picking you up. And after a while, if you hang in with this little group, you lose your sense of reality completely.'

Success is definitely not all it's cracked up to be. In fact, too much too soon, far from making you feel great about yourself, as you would be forgiven for assuming, can even *create* feelings of low self-esteem, because the acclaim from the outside world doesn't match how you feel about yourself on the inside – especially when you are just six, like Drew Barrymore was at the start of her career. And as for winning friends and influencing people, you are more likely to have to deal with the outside world's jealousy and cruelty. Brooke Shields talks in her memoir, *Down Came The Rain*, about being at a new school and taking her lunch tray to join a group of girls at a table, and all of them getting up as one and walking away from her without a word.

Or your partner might not feel secure with this new successful you hobnobbing with the rich and famous and being surrounded by fans. I love it when people ask for my autograph after a gig or tell me how much they love my CD, but I once had a boyfriend who would visibly twitch when that happened, or – when people asked about my career at dinner parties – would even say, 'Can we change the subject?' It made me almost dread people bringing it up, and it certainly spoiled my enjoyment of it. As for fame, as Meg Ryan said, 'Sometimes I'm like, "Oh God! I just want to buy some tampons!"' No wonder so many of us fear success at least as much as we fear failure.

HOT TIP

Stay grounded and focused on the reason you became an artist in the first place. As Gene Hackman said, 'I was trained to be an actor, not a star.'

MOVING ON UP

Success took me to her bosom like a maternal boa constrictor.
Noël Coward

Change, whether good or bad, is always scary. But even taking that into account, it does seem that there is a part of us that perversely wants to punish ourselves when we succeed, under-cutting our achievements with self-destructive behaviour – substance addiction, profligate spending habits, and/or bad relationships that suck our creative energy from us. Billie

Holiday is just one famous example who did all of the above. We all self-denigrate in varying degrees. How many times have you proudly proclaimed, 'Oh, it only cost me a fiver!' when someone has complimented you on your outfit? And it's not because you're proud of your bargain-hunting skills. It's because, for some nebulous unknown reason to do with ego, you can't handle the positive attention – unless of course you're like pianist Liberace, who used to hold out his clenched fists to his fans on his way to the stage so they could kiss his massive diamond rings. However, most of us wouldn't dream of responding to a compliment on a Rolex watch with, 'Oh, thanks. It cost me five grand!'

Speaking of which, another common means of self-sabotage, once your success translates into earning a living, is to get rid of your money as quickly as possible. But making money with a comma in it, perhaps even several commas, is not a licence to spend, spend, spend. Get yourself a good advisor to help you keep your feet on the ground. 'I do think it is vital to have someone you can trust and who believes in you looking after your interests,' says Veronica Henry. 'Who wants to be a flaky writer *and* a shit-hot businesswoman who can read the small print?' And don't necessarily go for the person with a star-studded roster. Instead, pick someone who will steer you away from imprudent 'feel-good' purchases.

Decide to invest a certain percentage of your income. And, since there is no such thing as a pension plan for artists, one of the first things you need to do is establish one. The arts are an unstable business, and you must protect yourself from the vagaries of the marketplace, when magical realist literature is hopelessly passé, or your music becomes yesterday's news, or, more frightening still, you get ill. Give yourself a financial cushion *before* you buy the vintage Porsche, or the new house with the gigantic mortgage.

Of course, this is easier said than done. When, after struggling for years, you suddenly come into money – money you've earned by plying the craft that once kept you in the poorhouse – it's a huge temptation to just go bonkers and give yourself all the things you've been denied for so long. It's like busting a diet, when you eat all the food in one afternoon that you've been depriving yourself of for months. But there are ways of curbing your excess – giving yourself an allowance, for example, or having in mind a certain amount that you let yourself spend on a long-coveted item. You can even arrange for your bank to pay a certain amount of spending money into your current account each month, and sweep anything over and above that amount into a savings account. And, of course, it goes without saying that you should know where your money is going at all times.

Part of the reason we may be so careless of our successes is that we are trained from childhood to fear the inevitable fall that *must* follow pride. In the fairy stories we grew up with (as well as in the press) the beautiful and the fortunate are always being punished – merely, it seems, for the terrible 'crime' of being beautiful and fortunate. Journalist Joseph Hooper confesses, 'I did have a fear of being successful young. I was so adapted to a sort of middling honourable survivorship, if I'd had some success I think I thought my ego . . . my whole body would explode. But now I feel to be successful older is good compensation for getting old.' In other words, if we *are* to be successful we must be willing to *pay* for it.

And maybe that's as it should be. As Bill Gates put it, 'Success is a lousy teacher.' I now think that if I'd been signed to the big label that approached me so early in my career – I mean, so early you couldn't even call it a career – I would not be as heartfelt a singer because I still had so much to learn. And I have benefited so much more through struggling than through anything that came easily to me.

I learned nothing from making my first demo, for example, because the planets were simply aligned in my favour, so it seemed, and it was a breeze. I just went in and told the engineer, who also happened to be the keyboardist, that I had $250 to spend so we'd better get it all done live with the bare minimum of post-production work. We did it all in a few hours. But I learned a hell of a lot from producing my first CD, which took a year of remixing, running out of money, and much correction of mistakes. Any success I had with it felt entirely deserved.

Veronica Henry was thirty-eight before she got a book deal. 'That seems old, but it now occurs to me that it was exactly the right age to become a novelist – because until then, what on earth did I have to write about?' she says. 'By then I had two children, had been married for over ten years and had seen a hundred different stories unfold over my dinner table, all with different resolutions. A book deal at twenty-two would have been, in the words of Arthur Daley's minder, a bit "previous". My work would have been shallow, superficial, meaningless, one-dimensional, because what did I know of life?'

Most successful writers do start off as something else – one rarely leaves school at eighteen to become an author. And those that do publish in their youth invariably don't come through with their second book. 'So before getting started, get a life; a perspective,' says Veronica. 'I am convinced now that if I had tried to do what I did any earlier, I would not have had a satisfactory product. But by my late thirties I had a pretty good idea of how the world worked, and therefore I could manipulate my characters convincingly.'

Biding your time until you have something to say is all well and good. But watch out for that pernicious part of your psyche that identifies yourself with your artistic expression, so that when your life changes for the better you no longer know who you are in your work. I remember once, in the early days of a great romance, wondering how I would be able to sing, I was so identified with my music persona of 'tragic, romantic heroine' – a persona, I might add, that my audience seemed to like, even if only because they wanted to root for me. After my singing 'Round Midnight' one night, someone in the crowd gasped, 'Baby, you must have *lived* that song!' And I am often hugged by complete strangers at the end of a particularly cathartic evening. Financially, too, I was so accustomed to seeing myself as a 'starving artist/abandoned waif' – not to mention being 'rewarded' for it by being taken care of by friends – I worried that people wouldn't love me any more if I got my hands on some money; if I was no longer 'me'.

The fact is, feeling successful takes some getting used to, so don't be surprised if you experience something like post-partum depression when it starts to happen. When I got my second manager, I felt completely undeserving. I kept thinking 'Why me?' as opposed to some of the other singers I knew who had been doing it a lot longer than I had. I remember when the feeling first hit me. I was in a friend's kitchen and a horrible guilt spread through me like a red wine stain seeping into a table-cloth. Surely it was a mistake, and surely, therefore, I was going to be punished. It took me months to tell people that I even had a manager, because it didn't feel real somehow, even though there I was on his website.

When I passed my driving test on the third attempt I had a similar feeling. I'd have nightmares in which I would accidentally retake my test and fail. When I'd explain to the examiner that it was a mistake and that I had actually already passed, he would say, 'I'm sorry, Tessa, but we will have to revoke your licence.'

The only way to get past this feeling is to be patient. Allow yourself time to get used to your achievements. Live with them for a bit. Get accustomed to this new successful you. Try it on for size and just allow yourself to witness your discomfort without letting it stop you. For example, it took me about six months to feel comfortable using my press quotes in my publicity material. It felt outrageously immodest. But I used them anyway. And I'm sure people *were* jealous. But I'm equally sure that as many people were happy for me, and those are the people to focus on. Now I am perfectly happy to use my good reviews, without feeling any guilt whatsoever. It's only someone's opinion, after all. And there is no need to feel guilty. That's buying into a kind of poverty consciousness. Don't worry, your success will not detract from or prevent anyone else's. It's not as if there's room for only one jazz singer/novelist/sculptor in the world.

It might help to remind yourself that art appreciation is all about taste, and just as there are people who think you're brilliant, there are also those who find you – yikes! – talentless. Two people in the same room can have entirely different opinions about your worth, and you should take neither extreme to heart. Ultimately, it's got to be your opinion that counts.

And while we're on the subject, try to avoid falling for your own publicity when you start to get some success. As actor Patrick Swayze said: 'If you live through the initial stage of fame and get past it, and remember that's not who you are. If you live past that, then you have a hope of maybe learning how to spell the word artist.' And Oprah Winfrey points out, 'If you come to fame not understanding who you are, it will define who you are.'

Art is a needy profession. You're putting yourself on the line emotionally, so winning praise and commanding attention can feel almost necessary to your survival – so much so that it can be tempting to surround yourself with a Greek chorus of fawning admirers. Naturally this isn't going to be good for you.

I remember assisting on a fashion shoot for kids one time and the photographer repeatedly exclaiming, 'You look so pretty!' Although the children were lapping it up, acclaim and attention for something as external as physical beauty is not the best recipe for developing your inner world. Nor is receiving attention for your success, or money.

And it works the other way too. Even the most successful artists get terrible reviews from journalists who have no idea how it feels to have invested months or years of blood, sweat and tears pouring out your soul on the thing. A bad review of your work is not a bad review of who you are. It might not even be that savvy about your work. One of my favourite reviews (I wish I had kept it, because it was so off the mark) was a slamming of Norah Jones, just before she got famous, saying she'd never get anywhere. As it happens I was at the very same concert that was being reviewed and was blown away by her talent.

And if you get a brilliant review, don't be disappointed if it doesn't lead to overnight acclaim. When I debuted in Los Angeles, I had a phenomenal review in the *Los Angeles Times* entitled 'An unsigned standout in a crowded field'. I was over the moon, not simply because it was a wonderful review but because I was sure that all the labels were going to be bashing down my front door with firemen's axes in their efforts to be the first to sign me. They probably didn't even see it. Or perhaps they just knew better than to believe the press. And the truth is, when you get down to it, it is only someone's opinion, after all. Take *everything* with a pinch of salt.

'Performers are not the most secure people in the world . . . In a very, very deep place, I'm secure but somewhere in there I need twenty thousand screaming people a night to feel normal. How sad is that?' said U2's Bono in an interview in *Vanity Fair*. However, at least from the outside, Bono appears to be an otherwise good role model for coping with success – his music has continued to develop and, in his spare time, he crusades for African debt relief. Sting, too, continues to develop as a musician and puts his fame to good use campaigning for the Brazilian rainforests.

HOT TIP
Be kind to everyone. Not only might the people you meet on the way up be the same ones you meet on the way down, but no matter how successful you are, you are no 'better' than anyone else. As Einstein said, 'Try not to become a man of success, but rather try to become a man of value.'

But good works aside, the fact that both Bono and Sting have continued to develop artistically suggests that neither of them are allowing their publicity or fans to lull them into complacency. Miles Davis also continued to push the envelope and develop as an artist, probably because people were too afraid of him to flatter him. Famously curmudgeonly, he was notorious for calling people on their efforts to curry favour with him. And who knows whether Gauguin would have been as good an artist if he had achieved success and acclaim before he went to Tahiti. The challenge is to not rest on your laurels and stop developing. Be like George Bernard Shaw, who said, 'I dread success. To have succeeded is to have finished one's business on earth, like the male spider, who is killed by the female the moment he has succeeded in his courtship. I like a state of continual becoming, with a goal in front and not behind.'

This is definitely something to watch out for. Surrounded by sycophants, you may find it hard to keep developing. When everyone wants to be your best friend, they may pump you up to the extent that you can't tell what's good or not. And being in a profession, the success of which depends on the opinions of others, can make you your own worst judge. As a fledgling journalist I would send off my articles with no idea at all if a piece was any good. In fact, I'd invariably think it was bad. It wasn't until the editor called and said they loved it that I would allow myself to think that it had any merit, and even then I wouldn't quite believe it until I saw it in print, unedited and exactly as I wrote it. This isn't entirely a bad thing. As Veronica Henry puts it, 'The minute you think you are good, then quit. It's the fear that keeps you going; the gut-wrenching anxiety and insecurity that drives you forward to write your best.'

When I first started composing music and lyrics I was so unsure of their worth that I used to sing them without announcing to the crowd they were mine. After enough people had come and asked me if certain songs I'd composed were on the CD, or they asked who wrote a song because they liked it so much, I felt braver about announcing they were mine at the outset. I also have 'music friends' who I run things by. When I was studying with Mark Murphy his encyclopaedic knowledge of practically every song ever written, and his talent for arranging, meant that he brought a wealth of knowledge and experience to his critiques, and when he really liked something I knew it must be good. And my friend Mansur, who hears all my arrangements and compositions at every stage of their development, is a constant inspiration. The fact that I respect them both as honest people and incredible musicians is huge.

It's also great to have someone who understands your work who you can run things past, who can tell you if you're going mad or, conversely and preferably, reassure you that you are on track. Audiences aren't always your best critics. While you want to please, you don't want to pander to them. For example, at the beginning of my career I often found myself doing vocal pyrotechnics that drew cheers from the crowd. When a musician friend called me on it, I said, 'But the audience loves it,' and he reminded me that, in music, the creative expression should always be true to the emotional message of the song. It's about the song itself, not how many notes you can fit into a bar.

That's not to say that there's anything wrong with enjoying your ability. I once saw jazz singer Cleo Laine live, and she revels in her technique. But so does her audience, because it is always in the service of the song, never just showing off. She is a perfect example of the fact that the purpose of technique is to make your expression better, rather than for its own sake – or, more accurately, for the sake of your ego. I suspect this holds true in all the arts.

ON TOP OF THE WORLD

I don't know the key to success,
but the key to failure is to try to please everyone.
Bill Cosby

If you're in any artistic profession to achieve fame, you need to think about why you are doing it in the first place. The nuisance is that in order to keep doing it, you ideally need to earn enough at it. However, there are degrees of fame, and areas where fame and 'acknowledgement' overlap. For example, I don't expect many of you have heard of Staffordshire-born cabaret singer Mabel Mercer, yet the fact that Frank Sinatra, Barbra Streisand, Ernest Hemingway, Gertrude Stein, F. Scott Fitzgerald, Cole Porter, and the Prince of Wales worshipped her qualifies her as a success. *Stereo Review* magazine gave her its first Award of Merit for 'outstanding contributions to the quality of American musical life', and in 1984 they officially renamed it the Mabel Mercer Award. Ronald Reagan presented her with the

Presidential Medal of Freedom – America's highest civilian honour – describing her as 'a singer's singer' and 'a living testament to the artfulness of the American song'.

On the other hand, fame seems to be a double-edged sword. As Brad Pitt put it, rather succinctly, 'Fame's a bitch, man.' Very few of those who achieve it seem to want it. 'Of all – hunger, misery, the incomprehension by the public – fame is by far the worst. It is the castigation of God by the artist,' said Pablo Picasso. 'I hate fame,' said Johnny Depp. Philip Seymour Hoffman says, 'Sometimes I'm uncomfortable with the level of fame I've got! It all depends on the day and what's going on. I don't desire any more fame. I don't need it.' Juliette Lewis says it is 'annoying'. Julia Roberts says, 'I don't think I realised that the cost of fame is that it's open season on every moment of your life.' I'm reminded of the story of King Midas who wished for everything he touched to turn to gold and then nearly died of starvation.

The other strange thing about success is that people who have it rarely *feel* successful. I remember once confiding in one of my singer friends that I felt envious of another singer and she said, 'Do you have any idea how many people are envious of *you*?' It woke me up to how silly I was being. But an editor friend of mine told me about a massively successful author who obsessively watched his position on the *New York Times* and *Wall Street Journal* best-seller lists and would go into paroxysms of rage and despair whenever anyone got ahead of him.

It seems that those people who enjoy their success the most are those for whom it is 'gravy'. Novelist Alaa El Aswany says, 'The reward I seek is from my writing only. I write because it makes me feel better. To express myself. To understand things. I had opportunities to make money. I was offered a job movie writing, but I refused. I like writing novels. I don't want to do something I wouldn't like. If you want to be a writer you must forget about fame and money.' He also went into it with no expectations. 'I met Naguib Mahfouz in a café once, just before he won the Nobel Prize for Literature. The waiter didn't recognise him. To him he was just an old man.'

In fact, Alaa's success has far exceeded his expectations. 'It has been unbelievable. I still get phone calls from fans every day, even after three years. I am constantly on TV. People recognise my face in the street, which I did not expect. I am treated like a celebrity. It is wonderful. I enjoy it,' he says. His family enjoys it too. 'My two little daughters love it when they see me on TV.'

HOT TIP
Keep your old friends around you. Keep up with them. Spend time with them. They will keep you real. As Drew Barrymore said: 'I'm not after fame and success and fortune and power. It's mostly that I want to have a good job and have good friends; that's the good stuff in life.'

Elizabeth Kostova, whose novel *The Historian* – a reworking of the Dracula tale – quickly outstripped even Dan Brown's best-selling *The Da Vinci Code* in America, clearly enjoys her success, claiming at a recent reading in New York that it was wonderful for anyone who'd just spent the last ten years in their pyjamas to experience such an enthusiastic response. As well she should. Just before her manuscript sold, she and her husband were debating whether they could afford a new pair of shoes.

But, in the end, how much you enjoy your success comes down to how you define it. 'I do get nervous about how many books I'll sell,' says Karen Quinn. 'I want my books to be successful financially so that the publisher will keep buying my work and I will get to keep writing.' She has no interest in being famous. 'My goal is to be commercially successful enough to make a living doing what I love,' she says. In the meantime, she already qualifies as a success according to her own definition of it: 'Being lucky enough to spend your days deeply involved with the work and the people you are most passionate about.'

'To laugh often and much; to win the respect of intelligent people and the affection of children; to earn the appreciation of honest critics and endure the betrayal of false friends; to appreciate beauty, to find the best in others; to leave the world a little better; whether by a healthy child, a garden patch or a redeemed social condition; to know even one life has breathed easier because you have lived. This is the meaning of success.' Anon. It is not just about the destination. You may never 'arrive'. It is about enjoying the process. As American socio-logist Charles Horton Cooley said, 'An artist cannot fail; it is a success to be one.'

How you can do it, too

1. Realise that success isn't always equated with financial prosperity. Poets don't make any money, but that doesn't mean they are not successful.
2. Give yourself time to get used to your success. Your new successful self will be something to get accustomed to in order for it to feel truly comfortable.
3. Take it as an affirmation of your talent if you get some success at the beginning even though it doesn't lead to anything right away. Use it to inspire you to keep going.
4. Keep pushing yourself to improve. Don't rest on your laurels.
5. Enjoy it, by all means, but don't fall for your own publicity. Just as you must learn to ignore the bad reviews, you should take with a pinch of salt the brilliant ones.
6. Stay centred. Don't get all your self-affirmation from the

outside world. Work on your inner world too.

7.   Be attentive to your partner. Of course, you hope they enjoy your success too but it can't be much fun being pushed aside by fans or being called 'Mr Kidman'. You may not be able to stop people approaching you, but you can make sure you introduce your partner by their full name and relationship to you. A light touch on their shoulder, holding hands and other physical demonstrations – short of tasteless snogging sessions – will help show the outside world that you care, as well as affirm to your partner that he or she is valued. The same principle goes for your friends.

8.   Stay focused on your own progress. Don't measure your success against other people's. Singer-saxophonist Sheila Cooper says, 'It would be nice to have Diana Krall's performance opportunities, but comparing my career to hers takes away what I am and what I have. I feel most fulfilled when I remember to be grateful for the gift of being able to make music.'

9.   Enjoy the process. 'When you actually get to number one, or whatever it is, it's different. It's the going for it that is fun,' said John Lennon. Fame isn't the goal – and 'success' could just mean earning enough from your craft that you can support yourself well enough to keep on doing it.

Success is to be measured not so much by the position that he has reached in life as by the obstacles which he has overcome.

Booker T. Washington

Chapter 11: Go Your Own Way: You Know Where You're Going

Be daring, be different, be impractical, be anything that will assert
integrity of purpose and imaginative vision against the play-it-safers,
the creatures of the commonplace, the slaves of the ordinary.

Cecil Beaton

Blimey! If you've got to this chapter, then you must really want
to follow your dream. Which is fantastic since, if you've read
this far, you already know what you're in for, unless you turn
out to be absolutely charmed. Throughout both careers as a
singer and a writer I have often despaired of how slowly I am
progressing to the next step; of the rejection, of feeling left
behind, of feeling envious, of the inability to take any step at *all*,
of the struggle for recognition. At other times I have been *afraid*
of moving too fast; of the attention; of inciting envy; of being
obsessive; of getting too big for my boots. I *often* feel 'too old'
or 'too late'. Or that I just can't carry on another second. And
as for talentless, well, of course!

But carry on you must. Because ultimately — whatever
happens, or doesn't happen — you won't regret it, even though
the road ahead may seem intolerably hard at times. As I've said
elsewhere, I can honestly say that even if I had been run over by
a bus only two days after I had taken that first step towards
becoming a singer, my last thought would have been, 'Well, at
least I started!' If I hadn't, I know my last thought would have

been, 'Damn! I didn't even try.' Whether you 'make it' or not, you will gain more than you realise just from the doing.

In my early teens, for example, instead of dancing, I used to sit on the sidelines judging other people's moves. Then, when I was seventeen, an amazingly beautiful girl at a party insisted my friend and I joined her on the dance floor. She turned out to be probably the worst dancer I have ever seen. But she was having such fun, it made me realise that this was the whole point of dancing. Not to look good, or even *think* about how it looks, but for its own sake, because it *feels* good – never mind some nit like me (too scared to do it herself, mind you) having a laugh about how you wave your arms. Now you can't drag me *off* the dance floor – even once when I was wearing a plaster cast up to my shoulder with my arm bent at the elbow.

And don't be intimidated by the brilliant dancers already out there. It is easy, and invariably discouraging, even downright destructive, to compare ourselves to others. One of the lessons of yoga is to compete with yourself only, and stay focused on your own development. On the other hand, everyone measures themselves against other people sometimes. If you can use it to your advantage – as in, 'If they can do it, so can I!' – then all well and good. Otherwise get a grip. Just think of actor-comedian Mike Myers, who said of himself: 'I'm basically a sexless geek. Look at me, I have pasty-white skin, I have acne scars and I'm five-foot-nothing. Does that sound like a real sexual dynamo to you?'

It's not about being the best dancer on the floor. It's about expressing *you*. One of the jobs of the artist is to find their own 'voice' – just as your idols did before you. No-one else can tell *your* story, and if you don't tell it, who will? When I first started listening to jazz, the idea of singing a Billie Holiday tune such as 'Detour Ahead' seemed like an abominable cheek. Who was *I* to sing one of the great Billie Holiday's songs? Then I realised that hundreds of singers sing the very same songs, and each has their own unique interpretation. To quote Broadway star Bernadette Peters, 'You've gotta be original, because if you're like someone else, what do they need you for?' The more I develop as a singer, and the more I know a song, the more it becomes the unique expression of *my* life experiences. My friend Mansur taught me to worry less about *how* I sound and more about *what* I am trying to say. It takes a lot of the pressure off.

Perfectionism is absolutely the enemy. Artist and illustrator Joseph Papin, who often drew on-scene with curious onlookers peeking over his shoulder, always said, 'Be bold, don't be afraid to draw in pen, and never apologise for a stroke.' If you are too hung up on being perfect, you will never finish – or possibly even start – anything. I write my lyrics in a notebook, so I have a record of how truly abominable and corny some of what later turn out to be my favourite songs have been in their early stages. Even the greatest artists feel inadequate to the task. Paul Klee wrote in his journal, 'I am still incapable of painting.' Van Gogh admitted, 'I am quite incapable of judging my own work. I can't see whether the sketches are good or bad.' Like them, *you* will not always be your best judge.

Expect your faith in yourself – in your talent, your drive, and even the universe – to wax and wane. Unshakeable confidence in your self is not a prerequisite for success. Moments of doubt are the shared currency of all artists. I don't mind admitting that I sometimes read fan mail to help me overcome my self-doubts. You can also use your self-doubts and fears to spur you on to greater things, to work harder on refining your craft. And when you're feeling confident, use that too. Catch the wave and ride it in, like a surfer. And remember, the harder and bigger the wave, the more fun you'll have.

The point is not how many times you fall off your surfboard, but your willingness to get back on again. If you've had a little taste of success in the beginning, that might keep you going for a while, but once bigger obstacles start presenting themselves, you may find yourself flagging. We've all heard the expression that it is darkest before the dawn, but most of us have also experienced the feeling 'surely it can't get any darker than this!' That's when you *really* have to bite the bullet and doggedly keep going, because the last thing you want to do is stop digging just before you reach the treasure.

One of the best ways to remind yourself of why you are a painter/writer/musician in the first place is to actually *do* it. You may not like the *idea* of getting on with something (procrastination is surely one of the deadly sins), but once you actually get started, I guarantee you will be in heaven. I can spend hours composing and arranging; I *never* get tired of performing; I even enjoy doing my vocal exercises. Likewise, novelist Karen Quinn loves the whole process of writing. 'It is exhilarating to me,' she says. 'I can sit at my desk and write for eight hours straight.'

But while you are getting utterly lost in pursuing this thing you love doing, try to balance it with making a living. Of course money is not your motivation for pursuing your creative dream. If it is, you're probably in for a rude awakening. Artists who hit the jackpot, like Nicole Kidman or JK Rowling, are rare. There's no reason why it *shouldn't* be you. Just don't bank on it and pawn the family jewels with a view to getting them back when you make it big. That may not happen.

In fact, focusing on making it big is probably the fastest road to depression. Success is just so random. Other people push in front of you, you're overlooked, you've just had your fifteenth rejection slip for your novel, someone with a quarter of your talent – or so your mum says – just got onto *Top of the Pops*. On top of that, your friends are angry with you for forgetting their birthdays because you were on a deadline; you're sick to death of not being able to afford to go out. Not to mention the fact that in choosing a career in which personal taste plays such a huge part, you are bound to get depressed, if only because not everybody's going to like you. Give yourself a break by focusing on what it is you love about it, rather than some end result.

As Harry Callahan said: 'To be a photographer, one must photograph. No amount of book learning, no checklist of seminars attended, can substitute for the simple act of making pictures. Experience is the best teacher of all. And for that, there are no guarantees that one will become an artist. Only the journey matters.' So go to it, and don't let anyone or anything keep you from trying to make your dream come true. As the saying goes, you don't regret the things you *do*, only the things you don't.

Each indecision brings its own delays and days are lost lamenting over lost days. What you can do or think you can do, begin it.

Goethe

Reading and Resources

Books are a fabulous resource, both for inspiration and solid information. As well as the books I have recommended here, I advise you to haunt the libraries and book shops and read as many books as you can around your particular creative discipline. I also suggest you read artists' biographies and memoirs. Not only will they inspire you, they will clearly show you how they achieved their success and steer you away from the mistakes that they made. The Internet is another wonderful resource. Do a search on your particular area. And if you feel you need support from like-minded artists, think about joining an Arts Anonymous group, a Twelve-step programme devoted to helping artists to get going and keep going. Visit: http://www.artsanonymous.org/

Anderson, Sheila E, *The Quotable Musician: From Bach to Tupac*, Watson-Guptill Publications, New York, 2003

Anderson, Sheila E, *How to Grow as a Musician: What All Musicians Must Know to Succeed*, Allworth Press, New York, 2005

Brande, Dorothea, *Becoming a Writer*, Pan, London, 1981

Bronson, Po, *What Should I Do With My Life?* Random House, New York, 2003

Cameron, Julia, *The Artist's Way: A Course in Discovering and Recovering Your Creative Self*, Pan Books, London, 1995

Carr, Ian, *Keith Jarrett: The Man and His Music*, Da Capo Press, New York, 1992

Davies, Miles and Troupe, Quincy, *Miles: The Autobiography*, Picador Books, New York, 1990

Fortgang, Laura Berman, *Living Your Best Life*, Thorsons HarperCollins, London, 2001

Fortgang, Laura Berman, *90 Days to a New Life Direction: Discover Your Own Blueprint for Success*, Piatkus Books, London, 2004

Forster, Mark, *Get Everything Done and Still Have Time to Play*, Help Yourself, London, 2000

Forster, Mark, *How to Make Your Dreams Come True*, Help Yourself, London, 2002

Graham, Martha, *Blood Memory*, Doubleday, New York, 1991

Jeffers, Susan, *Feel the Fear And Do It Anyway*, Vermilion, London, 1991

Lamott, Anne, *Bird by Bird : Some Instructions on Writing and Life*, Anchor Books, New York, 1995

Litvinoff, Sarah, *The Confidence Plan: Essential Steps to a New You*, BBC Books, London, 2004

Stead, C.K, (Ed), *Katherine Mansfield, The Letters and Journals: A Selection*, Penguin Twentieth Century Classics, London, 1977

Schwartz, Daylle Deanna, *The Real Deal: How to Get Signed to a Record Label*, Billboard Books, New York, 2002

Schwartz, Daylle Deanna, *Start and Run Your Own Record Label*, Billboard Books, New York, 2003

Scovel-Shinn, Florence, *The Game Of Life and How To Play It*, Vermilion, London, 2005

Sting, *Broken Music: Memoirs*, Simon & Schuster, London, 2003

Tracy, Brian, *Create Your Own Future: How to Master the 12 Critical Factors of Unlimited Success*, Wiley, New Jersey, 2002

Werner, Kenny, *Effortless Mastery*, Jamey Aebersold, New Albany, 1996

Woolf, Virginia, *A Passionate Apprentice: The Early Journals*, Pimlico, London, 2004

The Writers' and Artists' Yearbook, A&C Black, London, 2006

Acknowledgements

My undying gratitude to my literary agent Rebecca Strong who encouragingly midwifed this book into existence at every stage – a difficult birth! – and contributed to its manifestation way beyond the call of duty. I would also like to thank my great friend Jenny Seymore, who suggested I write the book in the first place. More undying gratitude to Jessica Papin, who provided her typing and considerable editing skills at the last minute when I broke my arm, and who generously shared her ideas and experiences. If it's true that everything happens for a reason, then getting to know Jessica is surely why I broke it in the first place. Thanks to my editors – to Judith Kendra for her belief in the book from the start, and to both Judith and Sue Lascelles for their enthusiasm once it was delivered. Thank you to Sarah Litvinoff who cheer-led my earliest efforts to become a writer, and was equally encouraging when I decided to become a singer. To Mansur Scott, my constant advisor and moral support, who is also always the first person to hear my compositions, lyrics and arrangements. To Mark Burford who encouraged me to be a singer – for which I am *sometimes* grateful. To my mother, who taught me how to sing when I was three. To my mentor and teacher Mark Murphy, who taught me how to be a jazz singer. To life coaches Laura Berman Fortgang, Mark Forster and Heike Bachmann for general inspiration. To the multitude of talented artists who generously allowed their stories to appear in these pages. Their stories were a great help to me personally, as I hope they will be to the readers of this book. And of course, to all my family and friends, near and far, who have patiently put up (and sometimes even joined in) with my bloodcurdling screams throughout the emotional roller coaster ride of pursuing my creative dreams.

The Game of Life & How to Play It
Winning Rules for Success and Happiness

Florence Scovel-Shinn

This classic guide has inspired at least three generations of people around the world to find a sense of purpose and belonging. It reveals that life is not a battle but a game – a game of giving and receiving. Whatever we send out into the world will eventually be returned to us, which means that if we give out love, we will be loved; but if we hate, we will in turn feel hatred. Through what we give and receive, we shape our reality.

Discover how your mind and its imaging faculty play a leading role in the game of life. Whatever you imagine or focus upon will sooner or later be experienced as part of your world. This book will show you how to change your circumstances, leave your regrets behind and create your own dazzling future.

Feel the Fear and Do It Anyway

How to Turn Your Fear and Indecision into Confidence and Action

Susan Jeffers

Whatever your anxieties, this worldwide bestseller will give you the insight and tools to vastly improve your ability to handle any given situation. You will learn to live your life the way you want – so you can move from a place of pain, paralysis and depression to one of power, energy and enthusiasm.

This inspiring modern classic has helped thousands turn their anger into love – and their indecision into action – with Susan Jeffers' simple but profound advice to 'Feel the fear and do it anyway'.